PHILIPPIANS

PHILIPPIANS

That every tongue should confess
that Jesus Christ is Lord
to the glory of God the Father
PHILIPPIANS 2:11

JOHN METCALFE

THE PUBLISHING TRUST
CHURCH ROAD, TYLERS GREEN, PENN, BUCKINGHAMSHIRE.

Printed and Published by
John Metcalfe Publishing Trust
Church Road, Tylers Green
Penn, Buckinghamshire

—

First Published October 1994

—

ISBN 1 870039 56 4

—

CONTENTS

INTRODUCTION

PHILIPPIANS

INTRODUCTION

WHEN Paul came to write the epistle to the Philippians, the gospel had spread by his ministry from Syria to Cyprus, north to Cilicia, to Galatia, Pisidia, Lycaonia, Phrygia, Pamphylia, through Asia, then Mysia, across the sea to Macedonia—thus reaching Europe—southward to Achia, seaward to Crete, and thence to the uttermost regions beyond.

Throughout all these countries the apostle had travelled, and sent his ministers, again and again, his gospel being the cause of the churches—or rather, of the *ecclesia*—being called out and established in the faith of Christ.

1

However, on the conclusion of his third and last evangelical journey, Paul had been arrested in Jerusalem, detained for two years at Caesarea, and sent in chains to Caesar's judgment at the centre of Empire.

This entailed a journey, under custody, by land and by sea, of at least two years' duration, following which the apostle was held in chains under house-arrest at Rome for something like another two years—the period of arrest thus far reaching into the fifth year—awaiting trial at Caesar's pleasure.

By this time the apostle was over fifty-five and probably nearer sixty years of age. It was now about thirty-five years since Christ had died, risen again, and ascended into heaven, to be seen on earth no more. The apostolate had aged, a new generation had arisen, and only the remaining elders remembered having seen Jesus after the flesh.

Already false teachers, purveying a damnable perversion of the gospel, were everywhere insinuating themselves, and particularly into those churches where Paul had once bestowed so much labour during the years of his liberty.

It was at such a time as this that the apostle, in chains at Rome, wrote the four letters which have come to be known as 'The Prison Epistles', namely, Ephesians, Philippians, Colossians and Philemon. At present our attention is drawn to the epistle to the Philippians.

Why was this epistle written? Who were the Philippians? When was 'the first day', mentioned in Phil. 1:5? What happened on that day? What took place between the first day 'until now', Phil. 1:5? What lay behind this epistle? To understand Philippians these preliminary and background questions must be addressed and answered satisfactorily.

THE BACKGROUND
OF PHILIPPIANS

THE BACKGROUND OF PHILIPPIANS

'From the first day until now', Phil. 1:5.

I

The Dawn of that Day

A S is the manner of the dawning of the day, this did not appear immediately over Philippi, but arose far distant, the first and faintest gleams suffusing the darkness of the horizon from the remotest reaches of the eastern sky. In fact that momentous dawn arose not in Macedonia, nor at all in Europe, but away beyond the sea in another continent, towards Asia, in the country of Mysia, towards the coastal town of Troas.

Paul, in those early days much exercised in spirit, was waiting in that town, together with certain of the brethren, seeking for direction in the will of the Lord on this the second of his great evangelical circuits in the preaching and teaching of the gospel.

Months before, the apostle had departed from Antioch, having chosen Silas to accompany him as he went through Syria and Cilicia, confirming the churches. Passing through

Lystra, Derbe, and Iconium, Paul called Timothy to minister to him as they went through the cities, each congregation being established in the faith, and increasing in numbers daily.

Thereafter the apostle and his company passed throughout Phrygia and Galatia. But for reasons unknown to them, the Holy Ghost forbad their going into Asia. Nevertheless they passed by outside the borders, having liberty to travel into Mysia, and, assuming that they were to evangelize in the north, they assayed to go into Bithynia.

But the Spirit suffered them not. Constrained in their spirit, twice rebuffed, they still sought. They did not give up. It was not that the Holy Ghost appeared to be leading them to where they should preach: it was more that he had increasingly made clear where they should not preach.

Shut up from the north and to the south, yet finding no witness against their travelling westward, always searching for the mind of the Spirit, they passed by Mysia, finally reaching the extremity of the land, facing the sea at Troas.

Now everything became clear. A vision appeared to Paul in the night. There stood a man of Macedonia, and prayed him, saying, 'Come over into Macedonia, and help us'. Immediately after Paul had seen the vision, the brethren determined to go into Macedonia, assuredly gathering that the Lord had called them to preach the gospel in that country across the sea.

A new land: a new people: and, moreover, a new continent: Europe. Here was an unprecedented opening to faith, to which the prohibitions of the Holy Ghost had first shut them up, so that nothing but the visionary door to the west stood open. For Europe, this visitation was the dayspring from on high.

Macedonia? But the Greeks, who sought after wisdom, had thought that the light of reason, the culture of civilization, natural or at least intuitive religion, besides the laws of creation, would have proved more than sufficient to find the unknown God, to his gratified satisfaction.

It was not in their mind that they were the people who sat in darkness, much less that they dwelt in the region and shadow of death. Nor could they remotely conceive that such light as they dreamed of—and in which they trusted—had neither reality nor existence in fact.

Yet upon this very nation, at once blind and in darkness, that sought him not, God had mercy; upon them the light was to shine; and it was towards their land that the probing fingers of the dawn arose from the east at the rising of what Paul was afterwards to describe as 'The first day', Phil. 1:5.

A vision appeared to Paul in the night. Well, it was night: 'And the light shone in the darkness, and the darkness comprehended it not.' For all the vaunting of human achievement, epitomized in the Greek culture, 'Darkness covered the earth, and gross darkness the people.'

As to the civilization of Greece, which humanity considered the centre of the arts and sciences: of architecture, sculpture, poetry, theatre, mathematics, geometry, trigonometry, physics, chemistry, literature, logic, philosophy, politics: what of it?

'Darkness was upon the face of the deep.' For here was a vision in the depths of the night, in which, for all their supposed enlightenment, the sole radiance was that of the pleading figure in the darkness: 'Help!' 'Come over and help us.'

Hitherto the Grecians had conquered the known world, establishing centres of culture world wide; they had made Greek to be the universal language, and this long before the Roman conquest. To the present day the Greek philosophy for mankind, politically, remains the dream of the idealistic ruler.

The very words Politics and Democracy are rooted in the Greek. Yet all these things found their genesis over five hundred years before the coming of Christ.

Unparalleled before or since, the Greek philosophers tower over the intellectual world: Socrates about 400 B.C., Plato around 350 B.C., Aristotle in the region of 325 B.C. These are the men who laid the foundations of philosophy, sheer giants to the veritable pygmies of latter days. In Mathematics too: Pythagorus about 525 B.C., Euclid around 300 B.C., Archimedes in 250 B.C.. Scientists withal: Thales *circa* 575 B.C., Hypocrates around 400 B.C., Democritus in the same era. Time fails to speak of the Greek Historians; Dramatists; Sculptors; Orators: all unsurpassed in their field.

Unsurpassed in Art: but art cannot tame the wild or corrupt passions; rather, in fact, debased, it becomes the stimulous of them. Unsurpassed in culture: but balanced education, once enshrined as man's holy grail, has quite failed to bring out the fruition of humanity, the pure love of learning, or the longed-for triumph of reason. Democracy: it has become degraded to a cynical appeal to the lowest common denominator by the richest manipulators: as if in practice the detached ideal could ever become a pure reality.

In fact history was soon to demonstrate the dark undercurrents that would expose and mock the theory, so that in every realm no sooner was the ideal propounded, than the demonstrable fact of the inability of its idealism to order mankind and nations aright gave it the lie.

Science? Medicine? To this day, medical science cannot halt age, cannot stop decay, cannot stay corruption, cannot prevent death: every aspiration and expectation, for all the vast funds poured into the attempt to realize its promises, remains, without a single exception, impaled upon the flaming sword turning every way to keep the way of the tree of life.

Philosophy? But philosophy could not answer the questions Why? Where? Whence? How? It could not reveal the unknown God: 'The world by wisdom knew not God.' It could not tell us where we came from, why we are here, where are we going. It could not address death, or expound eternity. It left its thinkers writhing on their death-beds, crying out, 'More light! More light!'

Philosophy? It is all groping in the dark, it is all the deceit of ignoring the infinite blackness to focus on some finite dying ember, as though that fading glimmer were the reality. Yet bare honesty, mere common sense, let alone philosophy, 'Frustrateth the tokens of the liars, and maketh diviners mad; turneth wise men backward, and maketh their knowledge foolish.'

Philosophy? Then why a desperate man sobbing in the darkness, chilled with fear, trembling with weakness, crying out as a frightened child in the night: 'Come over and help us'? Why? Because at its very apex the ascent of man had proved to be nothing but a delusive, doomed theory, without a basis in fact, or a witness in history.

II

The Day Itself

IN response to the heavenly vision, Paul and his companions immediately took shipping to Philippi, the chief city on the opposite, seaward, side of Macedonia, about eight miles inland. There they abode some time, although 'the first day' to which Paul alludes in Phil. 1:5, probably refers to the particular Sabbath on which he and his companions went out of the city to a river side, where prayer was wont to be made.

It appears that there was no synagogue in Philippi, since it was Paul's custom invariably to preach the gospel to the Jews first, then afterwards to the Gentiles. It should be noted that his being free in every synagogue to stand up and preach was a liberty to a Jew under law, far surpassing that of professing Christians in the denominations supposedly under the gospel!

However, there being no synagogue in Philippi, evidently the apostle spent certain days searching out the worshippers, and, on that particular Sabbath, found the place where prayer was offered up habitually by certain women—no mention is made of men—who resorted thither.

It was in this place that Paul and his brethren sat down, speaking to those few women—out of the whole population—who called on the name of the LORD.

Of those women with whom Paul and his companions sat down and spake, one is distinguished: 'A certain woman named

Lydia, a seller of purple, of the city of Thyatira.' Thyatira was built in the parts of the ancient kingdom of Lydia, believed to be founded by Lud, from whom its name was derived. He was descended directly from Shem, the second son of Noah, who passed through the flood in the ark.

Gen. 10:21,22, 'Unto Shem also, the father of all the children of Eber, the brother of Japheth the elder, even to him were children born. The children of Shem; Elam, and Asshur, and Arphaxad, and LUD, and Aram.' There being no letter 'y' in the Greek, Lydia's name—Ludia— indicates a female descendant of Lud, almost certainly of that ancient kingdom in the region of Thyatira.

So that although Lydia prayed with the women on the Sabbath, she was a Gentile, not a Jewess, and her sabbath-keeping would indicate that she submitted to the righteousness of the law given by Moses. She was a woman of ability, her business extending from Asia into Philippi, where she conducted her affairs in the merchandising of purple.

There is no mention of a husband; though she maintained her own household in that Macedonian city. Evidently she was a woman of independent and strong character, for, though there was no synagogue in Philippi, yet, knowing that God had chosen the Jews, and that to them were committed the sacred oracles, though it were with but so few women, she would keep the commandments of the law.

Hence she was at the riverside on that particular Sabbath day, in recognition that salvation was of the Jews. She met with the few—all women—who prayed, and, if so, for the coming and knowledge of the Messiah, which is called the Christ.

She prayed—for this is the nature of prayer—for better things to come; a better testament, founded upon better promises;

for a light to lighten the Gentiles, and the glory of his people Israel; she yearned for the coming of Christ, and looked for the grace of God in truth. And though they were so few, and all women, she could do no other, no, not for her very life, no, not even if she were quite alone.

This was the woman whom the Holy Ghost calls 'a worshipper', and, at that, before ever Paul and his companions, drawn by the vision from across the sea, in another continent, came that Sabbath to speak to the praying women in answer to the cry 'Come over and help us'.

Lydia heard Paul. But then so did the other women. But the work of God and the words of Paul marked out this woman. There was no doubt of the sheer conviction and overwhelming weight of the truth spoken by Paul. None could deny that. But Lydia attended to it: and the reason was 'the Lord opened her heart'.

Doubtless the judgment of all was carried: how could it not be? But there lay deep in the heart an interior enmity; a stubborn fear; a sullen rebellion, never so awakened as when 'Paul spake'.

Notwithstanding agreement of judgment and conscience, despite every intellectual prejudice and precedent being quite swept away, it was the heart that would neither submit nor yield. Except with Lydia, no mere hearer, but chosen of God. And this was the difference: 'Whose heart the Lord opened.'

This interior work of divine revelation, of spiritual creation, reached to depths of the soul utterly beyond the intellect, the understanding, the conscience, the judgment, the reason, and even the consciousness inwritten with the work of the law.

In Lydia the Lord from heaven reached down and within with a profound interior work that opened up the depths of her being, laying bare the heart itself with supernatural power from another dimension, incomprehensible to the senses. This lay beyond the power or reach of the will of man. It stood in the work of God alone, that is, in regeneration. 'Whose heart the Lord opened.'

It was not Lydia who opened her heart. It was the Lord who opened Lydia's heart. But to what end? That she should suppose herself wonderfully chosen for a marvellous work? That she should see herself standing on the threshold of a unique ministry to which she should presume herself singularly called?

Oh, no. She was a worshipper, not a modern evangelical! She feared God. She venerated the deity. She trembled at his word. She reverenced the Almighty.

Hence, if for no other reason, when the Lord opened her heart, she answered the cause with this effect, 'She attended unto the things'—things, mark it, things, which constituted parts of the whole of the doctrine of the gospel of the grace of Christ—'the things which were spoken of Paul.'

And if so, this was more than the dawning of the first day. It was the first day. For upon Lydia, first, the sun of righteousness arose with healing in his beams. And the effect of this was that 'She attended unto the things which were spoken of Paul', Acts 16:14.

Immediately she was baptized, and her house—for those were days when households were obedient to rule—and besought Paul and the brethren, saying, 'If ye have judged me to be faithful to the Lord, having entered my house, abide.' And she constrained them.

But as from Lydia's house they went to prayer—for they continued to go to prayer—whilst passing through the streets there followed them day by day a young woman with a spirit of divination, had in reputation for soothsaying, which brought her masters much gain. This woman cried after Paul and his companions continually, 'These men are the servants of the most high God, which show unto us the way of salvation'.

Sick of this unwanted testimony, after many days Paul, being grieved, turned himself about, and said to the spirit, 'I command thee in the name of Jesus Christ to come out of her'. And the spirit came out that same hour.

But when her masters saw this great deliverance of the demented woman, they knew that the hope of their gain was gone. Filled with enmity, hatred, and a spirit of revenge, they devised their plot, as their sort do to this day, and, catching hold of Paul and Silas, drew them to the marketplace to rouse up those who hang about in such places for the purpose.

There they held forth with grievous and bitter complaints, all no more than a pack of carefully constructed lies. Which is another thing this kind do even to the present hour.

Now nothing would suffice but for the crowd to drag these holy men before the magistrates, branding them as social undesirables and disturbers of the peace. At this, public opinion, or, perhaps, any students loafing about, roused to a frenzy over what was no more than a wholly fabricated accusation, howled for blood, as they heard the obviously proven charges: 'These men, being Jews, do exceedingly trouble our city'—being a Roman colony—'and teach customs, which are not lawful for us to receive, neither to observe, being Romans'.

At this dreadful headline, indignantly the equivalent of today's Rent-a-Crowd, that is, the multitude, rose up in common fury. Seeing this—catching the public mood—the magistrates went one better by rending off their clothes, for reasons best known to themselves and their advisors. Following this exhibition from the grave custodians of justice, nothing remained but the assuaging of the tumult by the lawless beating of the innocent.

Beaten, bloodied, and bruised, Paul and Silas were forthwith thrust into jail, being incarcerated by the jailor—in view of their heinous crimes—within the innermost dungeon, and, lest such monsters should escape, their feet were made fast in the stocks.

However, the common prisoners, clearly having been awed at sharing their prison with the very cream of their fraternity, were duly astounded to hear from behind the fast-bolted iron doors of the inner dungeon, whither the beaten and bloody arch-criminals had been hustled, the sound of sweet psalms, hymns, and spiritual songs arising with so divine and heavenly a melody, that, doubtless, they were all confounded. This continued unabated until midnight.

As midnight struck, and Paul and Silas were praying and singing praises unto God, suddenly there was a great earthquake. The very foundations of the prison were shaken, and that so mightily, that immediately all the doors were opened, followed by an extraordinary—if not supernatural—manifestation, namely, 'every one's bands were loosed', Acts 16:26.

Paul's answer to the jailor's cry has for several generations —the generations of evangelical decline—been used as the universal panacea by 'keen' Christians to 'tell others' how to be saved. 'Believe on the Lord Jesus Christ, and thou shalt be saved', Acts 16:31.

Yes, but the blind leaders of the blind totally ignore the preceding miracle of providence, the subsequent desperation of the jailor, the calling and inspiration of the apostle, and their own truncation of the text.

But if they do such things as this, it is certain evidence that they have had no experience of salvation themselves. Then how can they teach others the things of which they themselves are oblivious, and about which they are so blindly and obstinately perverse that they pretend that it is not so with them?

Moreover, the situation is not static: ours are the children's children of those who began in their rebellion what has proved to be a continuous decay, an increasing degeneration, ending with a final corruption even of text and version, above all the iniquity of their fathers. This accurately sums up the present lamentable—but unlamented—state of those in what is called —but called falsely—'evangelicalism' today.

First; they ignore the preceding miracle of providence. Well, they must, mustn't they, for when can *they* say that God broke into their unconverted lives with a divine providence so supernatural, so miraculous, so objective to themselves, and so obviously beyond the conniving and imaginings of man, that it simply *had* to be the work of God to bring them to repentance, thence to lead to saving faith?

And this miracle happened, mark—if they wish to quote the case of the Philippian jailor—in the darkness of the fall, and in the blackness of the jailor's ignorance, before he had the faintest glimmer of the reality of God's existence, or the least thought of the necessity of his own repentance.

Second; they conveniently dismiss the condition of the jailor, to whom the unique reply of the apostle was directed specifically in answer to the cry of his desperate and suicidal condition. No, rather they bandy about the word of God, light and airy as the wind, full of chaff, with their scraps of 'salvation' texts, persuading in the flesh every giggling schoolchild, every complacent somnambulist, every apathetic sceptic, and every unawakened sinner. As if there were the least resemblance between those whom they buttonhole in any convenient corner, and the purpose, work, and calling of God in the Philippian jailor.

16

But thus they think to wrap it up, as their fathers have done, and the noxious stream of American 'evangelists' have done, and done generation after generation, making every simple-minded fool who listens to their fabrication of texts twofold more the child of hell than themselves.

Consider the jailor. From deep sleep, secure and benign in his dreams, he was shaken awake by the trembling of the firm foundations, the shaking of the solid walls, the heaving of the stable floor, even the tipping of his fixed bed, all as if by a mighty avenging hand from heaven.

And now would not the melody of those sweet psalms, hymns, and spiritual songs, heard before through the iron door of the inner prison, ring in his conscience? Would not the finger of God touch his fearful memory, to prod it awake, to recall what, by now, all the city of Philippi knew only too well, if they would but remember these many days past: 'These men are the servants of the most high God, which show unto us the way of salvation', Acts 16:17?

Would not the scheming lies and the imagined plot of those covetous and iniquitous men who had for so long exploited the demented and possessed girl, now unfold before his face, nay, stare him in the face? Would not he, with the once frenzied multitude, realize at last the cynical manipulation of the instigators; the vapid capitulation of the rulers; the feeble gesturing of the magistrates; and the consequent unlawful assault upon the servants of the most high God?

And what of the jailor's own conduct? Knowing the un-righteousness of what had been done to Paul and Silas, he ignored it all. Fearing for his own job, puffing himself up to please both masters and fellows, without either pity or mercy —for justice had long since quit the scene—he himself had treated the apostles worse than decent men would treat a dog.

17

He had taken them, lacerated as they were, thrust them into the dungeon, driven home the stocks, slammed shut the iron door, and left them without food, water, sanitation, or the least attention to their ripped clothing, matted together with congealed blood and stuck fast in the wounds which criss-crossed their backs, and, indeed, their whole bodies. Treated as monsters, who was the monster? And what mercy could that monster expect, his own conscience bearing witness?

Blundering terrified from his sleep, stumbling out to the prison, as soon as the stricken man saw the prison doors open, he knew that all was lost. No pity for him under inexorable Roman law. Convinced that the prisoners had fled, he saw immediately that he was condemned, and that but one course was left open to him: 'He drew out his sword, and would have killed himself', Acts 16:27.

And what comparison is there between our modern version of 'Coming to Christ', dancing gaily as we go, and this man, and what he had done to the apostles of the Lord, besides the dreadful awakening that he had suffered, withal the terrible discovery that had shattered his very existence to the core, so that his drawn sword was in his hand, suicide in his heart, and the brink of eternity before his feet?

I say, what comparison between this man, and our indifferent, our giggling, our chaffy, our unawakened sleepers, to whom the light and airy 'evangelicals' of these latter days so glibly apply the text spoken to the jailor by Paul?

How came the jailor to Christ? It was Christ that came to the jailor. Hands gripping the sword, the point at his heart, in the act of falling upon the blade, suddenly out of the darkness of the open doors of the prison rang the voice of Paul, saying, 'Do thyself no harm: for we are all here', Acts 16:28. Straightway the jailor called for a light, and springing in, came trembling, trembling as a leaf, to fall prostrate before Paul and Silas.

18

Now, when these modern evangelical deceivers, or that series of American 'evangelists' who have plagued us for near a century and a half with their Arminian excuse for a 'gospel', their worldly showmanship for 'preaching', and their neo-psychology for being 'born-again', I say, when they can show that their 'converts' are at a point with the jailor in experience, then we will confess their right to apply the text which follows immediately.

Only, with this proviso: If it be preceded by the desperate and heart-rending cry, 'Sirs, what must I do to be saved?' Why, these modern creatures could not get so far as a 'Sir' before men, let alone a broken cry to God from the heart for salvation. But no less preceded what followed: 'Believe on the Lord Jesus Christ, and thou shalt be saved'!

Yet even this passage they cannot get right. Just as they diminish salvation, so they truncate the text. It reads in reality, 'Believe on the Lord Jesus Christ, and thou shalt be saved, *and thy house*', Acts 16:31. Here is the inspiration of the Holy Ghost, here the apostolic authority, here is the sending of preachers by the Lord from heaven, here is the very word of God.

But what we have suffered, and that to which we are come, is the substitution of platitudes for inspiration; and the exchange of a vile Greek text, with innumerable corrupt 'Modern' English versions, in place of the sound *Textus Receptus* and the tried and proven ancient landmark of the Authorized Version.

We have come to the rewarding of infidel ignorance with religious degrees. We have come to a kind of slick used-car salesmen, smooth chat-show hosts, in place of anointed and sent preachers. We have come to self-sent mediocrity in place of God-sent divinity. But it is still true: 'How shall they call on him in whom they have not believed? and how shall they

19

believe in him of whom they have not heard? and how shall they hear without a preacher? and how shall they preach, except they be sent?'

Sent, that is, by the Lord from heaven, as it is written, How beautiful upon the mountains are the feet of him that bringeth good tidings, that publisheth peace; that bringeth good tidings of good, that publisheth salvation; that saith unto Zion, Thy God reigneth! At these feet, the jailor now lay prostrate.

What beautiful feet, with such good tidings, brought by the Holy Ghost from the church at Antioch, and directed by a vision on the shores of Troas. One sees this scripture exactly fulfilled in the case of Paul with the Philippian jailor. Called; sent; brought; and attested. But this is certainly not fulfilled in the case of those whom we have suffered for generations.

With every syllable from the mouth of the apostle, the revelation of the Son of God from the Father in heaven pulsated with light in the inner man of the jailor. In the hidden man of his heart, the Holy Ghost bore infallible witness to salvation by faith in the glorified Lord Jesus Christ in heaven, who had first bled and died in the place of vicarious sacrificial substitution for the transgressor on earth.

Having justified the sinner by his blood; having reconciled him to God whilst he was yet an enemy; having in due time died for the ungodly; now from the glory by the will of the Father, by the word of his Son, echoed by the apostle, testified in the gospel, and witnessed by the Spirit on earth, salvation came to the Philippian jailor, and to his house, even by the commandment of the everlasting God and our Saviour Jesus Christ, brought home by the overwhelming, irresistible, sovereign power and grace of the Holy Ghost from heaven.

Now the jailor could not find water enough for joy, first to wash the terrible stripes and wounds which before he had left to fester, then all at once to be baptized, yes, and—subjection to the head of the house then being what it was—that his whole household should be baptized also. Overwhelmed with joy, rejoicing with all his own, he brought the apostles into his home and set meat before them. Thanksgiving, praise, and worship, arising from the heart sounded throughout, for the jailor rejoiced, believing in God with all his house.

In the morning the chastened magistrates—hearing too late that Paul and Silas possessed Roman citizenship—realizing the danger, came themselves and begged the apostles to be so helpful as to forget all and kindly leave the city as soon as possible.

Paul and Silas would oblige, yes, but not as though they thought it a light thing to have been beaten and imprisoned wrongfully by magistrates who had thrown the due processes of the law to the winds in order to pacify a tumult whipped up by the real criminals, namely, the perjured false accusers of Paul and Silas. Wherefore, heads held high, the evangelists take their time, passing by the chastened magistrates on their way back into the heart of the city, first to attend to the things of the Lord.

'And they went out of the prison, and entered into the house of Lydia: and when they had seen the brethren, they comforted them, and departed', Acts 16:40.

III

The Increase of that Day

'WHEN they had seen the brethren'? What brethren? Lydia had believed, and all her house. The jailor had believed, and all his house: but this was on that previous night. Hardly time to have met with Lydia's believing household. Then what 'brethren'?

Both Lydia's and the jailor's household had embraced Paul, and his gospel, knowing that he had not received this of man, neither by men, but by revelation of Jesus Christ. Both households had been baptized. Of this we are told, the jailor's household still damp from the outpoured water.

But what we are not told is whence the increase and fruitfulness that enabled Paul on the day of his departure to enter Lydia's house and summons 'the brethren'. What 'brethren' are these, that Paul could say 'Behold I, and the children which God hath given me'? And given with a birth and increase so prolific that the narrative cannot keep pace with it.

And why summons them? Was it that Paul and Silas might display their pitiful ill-treatment, show their stripes, expose their livid bruises, manifest their wounds, declare their imprisonment, speak of being in the stocks in the inner dungeon, and now—as if that were not injustice enough—seek the commiseration of the brethren upon their banishment from the city?

No. Not to do any of these things. Counting it all joy, disdaining even to mention their sufferings, rather, Paul called together the brethren that *he* might console *them*. 'They comforted them, and departed.' Now, *that* is the ministry.

And so it had been from 'the first day' till Paul and Silas left Philippi, even up to the time at which he wrote the epistle to the Philippians: 'until now', Phil. 1:5.

The ministry had been not in word only but in power also. Not alone in apostolic fervour but also in divine inworking. Not purely in mighty doctrine but also in holy fellowship. Not simply in suffering, affliction and adversity, but commensurately in the consolation of Christ, the comfort of love, the fellowship of the Spirit. Not in what they said, but in how they lived out what they said.

Not in precept only but in example primarily. What bowels of mercies, what issues of eternity, what revelation of the mystery; what heavenliness, what spirituality, what divinity, what mystery, what attendance of Father, Son, and Holy Ghost! Yet what humanity, what tender mercy, what lovingkindness.

This was the ministry: 'Even as a nurse cherisheth her children: so being affectionately desirous of you, we were willing to have imparted unto you, not the gospel of God only, but also our own souls, because ye were dear unto us.' From the first day until now.

How the breaking forth of the light of that heavenly day brought forth increase! First Lydia and her household. Then the jailor and his household. Next 'the brethren'.

All, all this since the darkness of the night so long ago, so far away, when, following weeks of being closed up and refused entry by the Holy Ghost, there had appeared a vision of a man of Macedonia praying to Paul 'Come over and help us'.

23

IV

Until Now

NOT once having been disobedient to the heavenly vision, now after so long a time, so many years, Paul in chains at Rome takes up his pen again, addressing not only those 'from the first day' but a host more: 'all the saints'—Oh, how they had grown and increased—'all the saints in Christ Jesus which are at Philippi.' And so many, that he must needs add 'With the bishops and deacons', a thing unique among the epistles.

And not only so, but now we discover Epaphroditus the messenger of the Philippians to Paul, Timotheus the messenger of Paul to the Philippians, women which laboured with Paul in the gospel, Clement also, and other, Paul's fellowlabourers, whose names are in the book of life. We find Euodias and Syntyche, we read of brethren dearly beloved and longed for. And how could it be otherwise?

For here was the house of God not made with hands. One house, but that one house as made manifest at Philippi. Here were all the saints that were in Philippi, all visibly united in one place. There were no other saints at Philippi, just as there was no other place in the entire city where the saints should be gathered together in one.

This was the *ecclesia*, the church of God, the one body gathered in visible unity at Philippi. There was one body: here was its manifestation at Philippi. They stood fast in one spirit, with one mind striving together for the faith of the

24

gospel; they all held the one unity, being perfectly joined together, without division, having the same mind, and the same judgment, and all speaking the same thing.

Far from being of the world, or worldly, the Philippians were separate from the world, pilgrims and strangers, the sons of God without rebuke, blameless and harmless, in the midst of a crooked and perverse nation, in the darkness of which they shone as lights in the world. As John the apostle put it 'We know that we are of God, and the whole world lieth in wickedness', I Jn. 5:19.

Here are two parties, and two parties only: 'we' and 'the whole world'. When *we* are thus united, in spirit, in heart, in mind, in judgment, and in fact, in one place; when we are united with all who are joined in one on the same basis and in the same unity in every place; when that unity is the consequence of submissive obedience to the apostle's authority, office, and ministry, whether in his presence, or much more in his absence; whether by him directly, or whether by Timothy, or whether by those sent subsequently in the same Spirit and submitting to the same truth, then, and only then, may we receive this epistle, or any text from this epistle, as though it had been sent to us, that is, addressed to us in principle, and in the same principle received by us. Then. But not till then.

In any and every other case it is a matter of misdirected mail; worse: it is the miserable offence of opening correspondence addressed to parties for whom it was not intended.

Nevertheless, when that same letter finds out those over the ages united under the same ministry, and holding the same faith as the original recipients, then the fruitfulness of the Philippian epistle will have increased above measure, beyond all that could have been asked or thought at the beginning.

Paul and Timotheus, slaves of Jesus Christ, wrote to all the saints which were at Philippi. Then, all the saints which were at Philippi were together in Philippi, not scattered in sects and denominations at different addresses all over the city.

The saints—mark that, they were saints; they were all saints; and there were no saints other than those saints at Philippi— the saints which were in Christ Jesus at Philippi were united together precisely because they were all obedient as one to the slaves of Jesus Christ, sent of Jesus Christ, that is, under one ministry sent to the whole church—the *ecclesia* in its entirety—from the heavenly, glorified, yet spiritually present Son of God.

The saints were all together with one accord in one place. This was true of every place: so that in their entire sum their common unity constituted the one *ecclesia*, the one house of God, the one body of Christ.

All had one mind, one spirit, one judgment. All owned the one ministry—not one employee voted in locally to preside over one place only: no such thing as *the* minister of *a* church exists in the new testament—but sent to all the saints, to the entire church in divine oneness: the apostolic ministry.

The saints looked for and required the marks of this ministry: but, looking, they actually discovered those marks, so clearly laid down and exemplified, particularly by Peter, John, and Paul. But more: they discovered the continuance of those marks in such as Timothy, Silas, and Titus.

They found the marks in those called of God, and sent under the apostolic word: they found them; they proved them: and hence their submission marked their unity in any one place, and their unity in every place.

Moreover, in the one church at Philippi existed a plurality of bishops and deacons. Not that there was one bishop over a number of churches: on the contrary, here was one church with a number of bishops. And deacons. None of whom elected themselves; none of whom was democratically voted in by a majority on Grecian political principles.

All of whom, bishops and deacons at Philippi—or anywhere else—were chosen and ordained to the work according to the word of God by the apostolic authority, and the authority of the apostolic ministry—and, in the absence of the apostle— according to the selfsame apostolic principles embodied in those called and sent of Christ from heaven till the end of the age.

Now, that is what we ought to have seen. It is what we should see. It is what should have been passed to us by previous generations. Yet it is what we shall see, the increase and growth of light being what it is, given obedience, not as in the apostle's presence only, but much more in his absence, even 'from the first day until now', Philippians 1:5.

THE CONTENT
OF PHILIPPIANS

THE CONTENT OF PHILIPPIANS

Part One
Philippians Ch. 1:1 to Ch. 2:11

'Let this mind be in you,
which was also in Christ Jesus', Phil. 2:5

E VEN in the case of the most doctrinal of the epistles, there
is always that which eludes the *écritoire* mentality of the
commentators. To the annoyed frustration of these gram-
marians, the matter obstinately refuses to submit to strict
classification. The text stubbornly eludes reduction to that
system of precise analysis so fundamental to the exactitude of
the philologist.

And if that be so of the particularly doctrinal epistles, it is
the more exemplified in the majority of the new testament
books.

These books reveal what I can only describe as a kind of
flowing spirituality; a fluid interchanging of doctrine, correction, admonition; of exhortation, consolation, comfort; of
interjection, exultation, intercession; of question, salutation,
parenthesis.

31

One discovers the unexpected, the inexplicable, the indefinable. One glimpses the mingling of humility with authority; of rhetoric with tenderness; of directness with allusion; of allegory with reasoning. And, all-pervading, one finds the most intense personal endearment suffusing the whole with the unmistakable fragrance of divine and everlasting love.

Whether particularly doctrinal, or broadly descriptive, more or less, this will be found to be true of all twenty-seven books of the new testament, just as much in the epistles as in the gospels. Nevertheless, there are those notable apostolic writings which soar sublimely above all categorization, defying mere intellectual analysis to a degree more pronounced than any others.

Among these are those few epistles which find their genesis neither in the saints' need, nor the apostle's burden. They are born of love, pure and unalloyed. There exists no other cause for their having been written.

Such epistles find their wellspring in the mystery of the deity: outpoured from the heavenly glory: issuing forth through the heart of Christ's servant as from a fountain unsealed.

In such distinct epistles the love of God seems to cascade out of eternity into time, out of heaven down to earth, out of the Godhead into the midst of the *ecclesia*, streaming unhindered from the throne of grace as a pure river of the water of life, clear as crystal, without course or boundary save that of the charting of the pen of the apostle.

The genesis and the issue of such divine and living water defies all intellectual categorization: every sentence spills liquid and joyous with life-giving, heart-enlarging, soul-ravishing testimony to its heavenly, eternal, spiritual, divine and mysterious source: 'For God is my record, how greatly I long after you all in the bowels of Jesus Christ.'

God is my record. My record. How greatly, greatly I long, long after you all. All. In the bowels of Jesus Christ. In the bowels of Jesus Christ? Who else would dare say such a thing? Here is the essence of such writings as those of which I have spoken. It is from the epistle to the Philippians.

In the first two verses Paul announces the correspondents and their blessing. Of the thirteen epistles bearing his name, Philippians is one of only four in which he does not invoke his apostolic office; it is also one of six in which he associates Timothy with him in the authorship of the epistle.

As to his not invoking the title 'apostle' in Philippians, here there is no need. Nothing to correct; nothing to instruct; only love to impart, and thanksgiving to convey.

Regarding his association of Timothy with him in the authorship, Paul the aged knew that his days were numbered, the time of his departure was at hand, and it was no thought of his—no counsel of the deity—that the saints should be without the continuance of the apostolic ministry, or that the *ecclesia* of God should ever lack those who would in turn fulfil the office then borne by Timothy or Titus, as long as time should endure.

Unique to Philippians is its dedication not only to the saints, but also to the bishops and deacons. Whereas bishops are associated in a certain place with elders—though distinct from them—in only one other passage are the offices of bishop and deacon mentioned together: that is, in the first pastoral epistle to Timothy.

There Paul commands Timothy in his absence to ordain bishops and deacons at Ephesus. These offices were appointed, not elected. They were ordained by those ministers of the gospel sent to all the churches—as opposed to any conception of a minister serving in one church alone—and both bishops and deacons were chosen according to the apostolic commandment, and by nothing else, and no other rule, whatsoever.

Furthermore, there was no such thing as one bishop over a plurality of churches in a diocese. In fact in the entire new testament, and over the whole apostolic period, and throughout the total scriptural history of the church, there was no such thing as a diocese at all.

As you may plainly read, what existed by divine authority was a plurality of bishops within any one given church, and, likewise, a suited number of deacons ordained by the apostolic ministry in each distinct assembly.

Over all the assemblies, as one, the apostolic ministry—in the absence of the unique twelve apostles, and in submission to their concluded writings—such as Timothy, Titus and others their successors, were to continue the preaching, teaching, ordination, and administration as it was from the beginning.

With the future prospect of the departure of the apostles in mind we see the wisdom of the introduction 'Paul *and* Timotheus, the slaves of Jesus Christ, to all the saints in Christ Jesus which are at Philippi, with the bishops and deacons.'

This was of God, when everything was of God. Everything was of God, when nothing was of man. And so it obtained under the apostles, and so it should have continued under those sent after their decease, unchanged to the end of time.

The Philippians were saints by grace, chosen, born of God the Father, who had called those who had never called upon him. This grace had chosen them in Christ Jesus before the world began. This grace had redeemed them by the blood and sacrifice of Jesus Christ when that blood was shed in the midst of time or ever they so much as knew whether either Saviour or sacrifice existed. And the same grace had arrested them and converted them by the revelation of Jesus Christ whilst amidst of a heedless career to destruction, out of this world, through death, and into eternity.

Such grace from God the Father was pronounced by the ascended Head, the Lord Jesus Christ, preaching peace from the throne of the heavenly glory by the invisible, inward, but very real Holy Ghost to their hearts here below upon the earth. What grace! What peace!

'Grace unto you, and peace, from God our Father, and the Lord Jesus Christ.' That was what had been preached by the apostles, sent of God, attested by the Holy Ghost, from the beginning at Philippi. That was how the church at Philippi had come into existence.

In the next nine verses—verses 3 to 11—Paul declares his remembrance of, confidence in, witness to, and prayer for, the saints at Philippi. Paul remembered the Philippians 'always', and, as often, 'in every prayer of mine for you making request with joy.'

What daily hours, what unceasing vigil, what disciplined time this indicates: and if this 'always' and in 'every prayer' be true of the Philippians, it was no less true for each assembly of the saints, and for the entire assembly of God: 'That which cometh upon me daily, the care of all the churches', II Cor. 11:28. Hours, daily hours, nightly hours, whole days and nights, given over to prayer. Of this, Paul's continual requests and supplications for the Philippians bear witness.

'Behold, he prayeth', Acts 9:11. This was heaven's testimony to that devout life, largeness of heart, greatness of faith, love for all the saints, zeal for the testimony, and breathing towards God, characteristic of Paul's entire service and ministry.

However, in the Philippians' case, this continuous request was not for their correction, nor for their instruction, but it sprang from that which welled up in his heart for joy at their fellowship and union in the faith.

This brought divine consolation to the apostle—no small comfort in his present affliction at such distance, and for so long, from their presence—their fellowship was in the evangel! It was grounded in the gospel, the doctrine of Christ, in the interior power and experience of the tremendous and awesome doctrines which constitute that perceived body of truth.

This fellowship in the evangel was the cause of that divine, spiritual, and heavenly confidence of Paul that the work begun in them was of God: and if so, that it would surely continue—even in his absence—until the day of Jesus Christ.

Having revealed wherein true fellowship was enshrined, and that which constituted its inmost bond, besides that which compassed it about as with the walls of salvation, the apostle proceeds from their 'fellowship in the gospel', verse 5, to their 'defence and confirmation of the gospel', verse 7.

This vigilance of theirs was written in Paul's heart. This was sure evidence that they had received the word from him, not in word only, but in power also: the oil of gladness had been poured from the glory through the golden pipe of his apostolic ministry even into their hearts, so that they were 'all partakers of my grace', verse 7.

Oh, what divine bonds! What an unspeakable mystery of fellowship! What spiritual union between the sent apostle and the receiving saints, revealed by these words, 'Ye all are partakers of *my* grace.'

With their whole heart, from the depths of their being, the Philippians could say, 'How beautiful upon the mountains are the feet of him that bringeth good tidings, that publisheth peace; that bringeth good tidings of good, that publisheth salvation; that saith unto Zion, Thy God reigneth!' Isa. 52:7.

And again, Nahum 1:15, 'Behold upon the mountains the feet of him that bringeth good tidings, that publisheth peace! O Judah, keep thy solemn feasts, perform thy vows: for the wicked shall no more pass through thee; he is utterly cut off.'

This was the very doctrine, applicable to the end of the age, predicated in Romans 10:14,15. Yes, predicated, but the heavenly glory of the mystic union of its actual experience, who can tell? The Philippians could tell.

And Paul rested in that union, unutterable, divine: in the bowels of Jesus Christ—Oh, who can reach the profundity of these words?—'I long after you all in the bowels of Jesus Christ.'

Hence he proceeds to his prayer on their behalf. It is not a prayer for judgment apart from love: it is a prayer for the judgment of love. It is not a prayer for righteousness distinct from love: it is a prayer for righteousness in love. It is not a prayer for indulgence of offence: it is a prayer to be without offence. It is not a prayer for a moment of decision: it is a prayer for a lifetime of grace. It is not a prayer in the singular: it is a prayer in the plural. It is not a prayer for the individual: it is a prayer for the church. Hear this prayer:

> 'And this I pray, that yet your love
>   may more and more abound
> in knowledge and discernment clear,
>   and in all judgment sound;
>
> That those things which are excellent
>   approve thereby may ye;
> that till the day of Christ ye might
>   sincere and blameless be;
>
> Filled with the fruits of righteousness
>   by Jesus Christ always,
> that ye may render unto God
>   the glory and the praise.'

Next follows Paul's testimony, its consequences, and his expectation, Ch. 1:12-26. The first part, the witness which the apostle bears to the dealings of God which many would have considered to have been against him, and the providences which to most would appear to have run clean contrary to his continuing in the ministry, the apostle shows in quite another light than that which seemed to shine on the surface.

True, he was in chains; yes, he had been forced to take many tedious and adverse journeys as a prisoner; certainly, he had been shipwrecked; it was right that he had been marooned, and, yes, this had been followed by further imprisonment, the whole lasting for some five long years. All this, I say, which the majority would certainly take for cross providences showing the turning away of God's countenance, Paul now demonstrates to have been for the furtherance of the gospel!

But not only were his cross and adverse providences generally misinterpreted: even more misunderstood appeared to have been Paul's explanation of his manacles, chains, bonds, and their effect, verses 12-20. And that is true to this day.

It has suited the erroneous to misconstrue Paul's words in Phil. 1:12-20. Those who will misunderstand this passage generally want to misunderstand it, in order that they can justify the heretical divisions and contradictory gospels, emanating from their own various parties and divisions multiplying throughout Christendom.

In this way they attempt to draw Paul in on their side as if what he were saying was that so long as Christ was preached, no matter the Babel of confusing voices, despite the absurdity of irreconcilable contradictions, for all the multiplying heretical divisions each preposterously professing one faith, that was just fine; carry on: Philippians 1:12-20 justifies everything!

However the apostle walked in light, not darkness; he savoured truth, not error; he dwelt in Zion, not Babel; he was a son of righteousness, not disobedience, and hence the smallest child can see plainly what quite eludes the sight of those who wish to pervert the scripture to justify their own and others' unrighteousness: Paul simply couldn't—in his very nature he couldn't—he couldn't have meant what they say he meant. Well then, what did he mean? It is this that we are to resolve.

'But I would ye should understand, brethren', writes Paul, 1:12, 'that the things which have happened unto me have fallen out rather unto the furtherance of the gospel.' But why would he have them to understand that? And just what had fallen out rather unto the furtherance of the gospel? Why, some five years in custody, or more, held in chains, and much of it either in prison or under house-arrest.

And what would Paul's multitude of enemies in religion and throughout the churches make of that? 'Oh, he's come to nothing.' 'Oh, it was all a flash in the pan.' 'Paul? Oh yes, he fell you know; lot of rumours, no smoke without fire: besides, God was against him—five years in prison you know; all his work in ruins—his real motive and character came to light, the Authorities soon found out: still in chains, of course.' 'Paul? Finished. God judged him; been in prison for years. Old man now, you know.'

Not at all: God had testified, and the Spirit had borne witness of Christ and his gospel, by Paul's mouth, before kings and rulers at Caesarea, a thing impossible had the apostle not been under arrest.

Not at all: God had testified by Paul throughout the long journey to Rome, saving the whole ship's company for Paul's sake, whilst fulfilling every prophecy at his mouth, and working apostolic miracles by his hands, throughout all the island of Malta.

Not at all: God caused his power so to rest upon the apostle at Rome, that he had been granted licence openly to receive all whom he would into his own hired house, though he was chained, testifying fully of the grace of our Lord Jesus Christ.

Not at all: the witness of the apostle Paul at Rome inspired and elevated the testimony of Christ throughout the entire centre of the empire, to the very throne of Caesar, emboldening all, so that where Christ had never been named, and where none had dared to name him, *Paul's* name and repute, withal his holy boldness, had stirred up such an enquiry about *himself*, that news of his own explanation had caused *Christ's* name to sound throughout all the palace, thence to echo to the uttermost suburbs of the city.

Now, slanderers; now, talebearers; now, evil speakers: what have you to say to that? For the things that happened unto him fell out rather to the *furtherance* of the gospel. And *without* these things the gospel would never have gone either so far or so wide.

'And many brethren in the Lord, waxing confident by my bonds, are much more bold to speak the word without fear.' Yet, astonishingly, 'Some indeed preach Christ even of envy and strife.' The most remarkable feature of these verses—Ch. 1:14-18—is seen in the way in which Paul himself was the catalyst for the preaching—of both kinds—provoked by his presence at Rome.

Here, the preaching of others is seen to be a reaction to *him*, rather than to *Christ*. Paul himself was the cause of the provocation to preach Christ, and at that, in opposing ways by two opposite parties. The failure to see this obscures the whole meaning of the passage.

Observe: whether brethren in Christ or not—God knoweth —two classes of persons were provoked into preaching Christ by the presence of the apostle: 'Some preach Christ even of envy and strife; and some also of good will', v.15. 'The one of contention, not sincerely', 'The other of love', v.16,17. Love, yes, but it was love for *Paul*: 'the other of love, knowing that *I* am set for the defence of the gospel.'

A twofold reaction to Paul provoked opposite effects. This is not to speak of the end result of Christ being preached. It is to demonstrate that the different motives of others for preaching Christ were on the one hand the desire to hurt Paul, and on the other the desire to help him.

On the one hand the desire to hurt Paul? Yes, it says so: 'The one preach Christ of contention.' Why, Paul? 'Supposing *to add affliction* to my bonds.' That was their motive. 'But the other of love, knowing *that I* am set for the defence of the gospel.' And that was the opposite motive. But the catalyst of both, you see, was Paul: reaction to Paul.

Very well, what was *Paul's* response to this, and, more importantly, *why* did he so respond? It is just here that so much misunderstanding arises. What was Paul's response to this disparate preaching of Christ? Why, he rejoiced in both kinds! 'What then? notwithstanding, every way, whether in pretence, or in truth, Christ is preached: and I therein do rejoice, and will rejoice', 1:18.

From this the impossible is concluded by the ignorant. As if Paul could joy—*as an end in itself*—in a false Christ, falsely preached, by false preachers, through a false gospel, falsely employed. Would he rejoice in that? You say, But it says he rejoiced in it. But you must see what he meant: you must see his reason for the joy of which he speaks.

His rejoicing was not for such preaching *in and of itself*. That would have contradicted a thousand places in the new testament, not to say the very context, for you must bear in mind that he had only just finished saying that he was set for the *defence* of *the* gospel, not its abuse and perversion.

41

Then how could he rejoice in *that*—I mean that abuse and perversion—just as much as he rejoiced in the *sincere* preaching of Christ? The two things are not compatible.

I told you that it was essential to see that Paul—and rightly—was the central figure. He was the catalyst of both kinds of preaching *neither of which had occurred before*. The preaching, I showed you clearly from the context, *was a reaction to Paul*. But—whatever the preaching—it was the *result* that gave him joy. Not the preaching in and of itself, for good or ill, but—whether good or ill—*for the effect either would have*.

Do you find that difficult to accept? Do you still think Paul would have contradicted his whole testimony by approving that which he always and everywhere else deplored? His rejoicing was not *primarily* in the preaching as such: it was in the *effect* that this preaching—of either kind—would have: 'For I know that *this*'—*this*, this *preaching*; either way: *this*—'shall turn to my salvation through your prayer, and the supply of the Spirit of Jesus Christ', v.19.

To your salvation? Salvation from what, Paul? Why, salvation from execution by Ceasar's sentence of death against him. The Philippians' prayer for whom, Paul? Why, prayer for Paul *himself* when he stood up at Caesar's tribunal to testify to the cause of his bonds in Christ.

'Through your prayer, and the supply of the Spirit of Jesus Christ', 1:19. But the supply of the Spirit of Jesus Christ to whom? To those preachers? Of course not: *to Paul*. But when? When? Why, when he was brought before the great assize of Caesar's judgment, to testify of the reason for his bonds. *That* mattered more than anything; because *that* would be preaching that was *apostolic*; preaching which eclipsing all other, though that other—of both kinds—had stirred up the interest leading to the very moment, when the principal should testify for himself of the answer to every enquiry, and that before the very throne of Caesar.

42

That end effect was why Paul rejoiced in all the clamour; all the diverse kinds of preaching by others; all the consequent enquiry; all the division of opinion about himself; all the raising of questions about his accusation. Already, this was noised abroad, so that not only the whole city, but all Caesar's palace, and, if so, Caesar himself, would in consequence want to know in all this confliction of rumour and lack of authoritative declaration just what *was* this gospel; exactly *who* was this Christ? Only *one* man could answer that.

I say, only one man could answer that, and, for the tremendous occasion on which he should be summoned to do so, that same man—the apostle Paul—humbly entreats 'Your prayer, and the supply of the Spirit of Jesus Christ.'

Why? That he might be—if the will of the Lord should so ordain—acquitted by Caesar, after having delivered *such* a testimony. Then, delivered out of the mouth of the lion, that it might please the Lord to set him free again to preach and teach the gospel once more, even to his dearly beloved brethren at Philippi, and to the regions beyond.

It was this that he called 'my salvation', v.19. What would lead to this salvation, through such a testimony, would be the curiosity, the speculation, the enquiry everywhere raised by all this talking, for and against, all this preaching, envious and loving, where, before, even the name of Christ had never been heard.

Now the question was, What was the defence of this man who had stirred up so much clamour? What had the man, this unique man, the man so singularly sent to declare the mystery of Christ, what had this man to say for *himself?* That was the question. And it was Caesar's question.

Yet though Paul hoped that the interest raised in Caesar's palace—by whatever contradictory means—concerning this virtually unknown Christ, would, through the Philippians' prayers beforehand, and the Spirit's supply at the time, result in his salvation from the threat of execution. Nevertheless should it prove otherwise, he would be moved not one whit.

Whether he was acquitted and lived, or whether he was condemned and died, neither prospect would have the least influence upon his testimony, or upon the witness he trusted to be enabled to bear at Caesar's tribunal. Such considerations —mere life or death—had no influence, absolutely no influence —and if not, then how much less any earthly or worldly consideration—no influence upon the single eye of the apostle.

'According to my earnest expectation and my hope, that in nothing I shall be ashamed'—before Caesar—'but that with all boldness, as always, so now also Christ shall be magnified in my body, whether by life, or by death', Phil. 1:20.

For Paul there was nothing in this life, in earthly relationships, or in the whole world, to which he was not already dead. 'I am crucified with Christ', he says; and again, 'God forbid that I should glory, save in the cross of our Lord Jesus Christ, by which the world is crucified unto me, and I unto the world.' Or, as he says here, 'For to me to live is Christ, and to die is gain.'

Only one cause existed on earth, in time, through this present world, or in the life which he now lived in the flesh: the preaching of the gospel; the edification of the saints; the care of the churches; the unity of the *ecclesia*. But what affliction, what suffering, what persecution, what maligning, attended this holy pathway! 'To depart, and be with Christ is better.' Yes, Paul, but how does the balance tilt? 'Nevertheless, to abide in the flesh is more needful for you.'

Having therefore this confidence, he knew that he should abide and continue with the *ecclesia*, with all the faithful brethren, for their furtherance and joy of faith: that their rejoicing might be the more abundant in Jesus Christ by Paul's salvation from the power of the sword at the tribunal of Caesar, so that he should come to Philippi again. And so it came to pass.

But, in passing, observe that this is the spirit, and the only spirit, that can ever justify the title 'minister of Christ'. This title predicates a ministry set apart by such a heavenly ordination, such a spiritual qualification, such a divine degree, that not only emulates the very chiefest of the apostles in uprightness of stature, but which proves itself by the ultimate test of the sword of judgment, before which it has the same unflinching witness of faith and love, life and death, heart and experience. Beneath this, none can possibly descend, and rightly retain the name, 'minister of Christ'.

In the closing verses of Chapter 1, from verses 27 to 30, Paul exhorts the Philippians to a becoming conversation in the midst of adversaries and persecutors, sufferings and conflict. This was their common lot with the apostle, whose clear testimony to the gospel of the grace of Christ—which they had received and obeyed—brought down all this affliction and enmity upon his own and upon their head.

Observe therefore that it is the witness to the gospel, the evangel properly so-called, a witness from the heart, with the mouth, by the life, and in the spirit, which brought about all the trials peculiar to the apostle. It is equally important to notice that this is just as true of the saints distinguished by submission to this true evangel, and kept in obedience to that faithful and sent apostolic ministry.

Here I would remind you, 1:17, that Paul was 'Set for the defence of the gospel'. If so, it needed defending. From whom? From what? Evidently, from the errors of the contenders.

45

Who are these? The entire religious world, apart from the saints gathered under the apostolic ministry: 'For we know that we are of God, and the whole world lieth in wickedness', I Jn. 5:19. 'They are of the world: therefore speak they of the world, and the world heareth them. We are of God: he that knoweth God heareth us; he that is not of God heareth not us. Hereby know we the spirit of truth, and the spirit of error', I Jn. 4:5,6.

It was for the defence of the gospel against the errors of these, and the world that embraced them, that the apostle was set: for this, they hated him: 'As then he that was born after the flesh persecuted him that was born after the Spirit, so now', Gal. 4:29.

In like manner—Ch. 1:7—Paul stood for the confirmation of the gospel. If so, that gospel needed confirming. But confirming to whom? To the saints. To establish them against every specious imitation offered as an alternative.

For there are no alternatives, although the false church and the religious world were even then full of invented alternatives. But there is one true gospel, and the apostolic ministry confirms its precise nature, in the parts, in the sum of the parts, and in the proportion and balance of each part the one to the other, thus comprising the sum of that evangel called, The doctrine of Christ.

If any man, or church, move from this, they have apostatized. 'I marvel that ye are so soon removed from him that called you into the grace of Christ unto another gospel: which is not another; but there be some that trouble you, and would pervert the gospel of Christ', Gal. 1:6,7.

But I would beseech you to keep in mind that Paul was set for the *confirmation* as well as the *defence* of the gospel: *the* gospel, not any number of gospels. And if *the* gospel, then of *one*

Christ, not a variety of contending opinions about him: 'One Lord, one faith, one baptism.' 'I *am* the truth', saith he, and that truth, in every part, in the sum of all the parts in their proper place and balance, that truth, I say, is called *the* gospel.

It, *it*, is the power of God unto salvation, Rom. 1:16, and, in the beginning and from it, this one gospel was preached and taught by ministers called, prepared, ordained, and sent by Christ, and subject to his apostles, even to this latest day. As to the character of those who received this one, this only, this dogmatic, this singular gospel, this saving truth, why, such a description appears in Rom. 6:17, 'Ye have obeyed from the heart that form of doctrine which was delivered you.'

However, so to obey, so to submit, so to be ordered under the apostolic ministry—in doctrine, fellowship, discipline and ordinance—brought contentious circumstances, and created a hostile environment. For when they were 'Standing fast in one spirit, with one mind striving together for the faith of the gospel', it was needful for the apostle to exhort them to be 'in nothing terrified by their adversaries', 1:27,28.

Why should the saints not be terrified by these adversaries? Because the saints' love in one spirit and one mind for the one gospel on the one hand, and their adversaries' denial of that spirit, mind and gospel on the other, was to those adversaries 'an evident token of perdition', but to the Philippians 'of salvation, and that of God', 1:28.

Thus the brethren shared in one with the apostle in all his sufferings and conflict for the truth of Christ enshrined in the evangel. Hence the admonition:

> 'Let all your conversation with
>   Christ's gospel well agree;
> that I may of you hear, though I
>   should come, or absent be:

That striving for the gospel's faith
   ye with one mind abide,
and in one spirit; by your foes
   in nothing terrified:

Which of perdition evident
   a token doth afford
unto them all: but unto you
   salvation sent from God.

For in behalf of Christ, to you
   'tis given to partake
not only of belief in him,
   but suff'ring for his sake;

Whilst having that same conflict which
   in me at first ye saw,
and now do hear to be in me,
   a token true and sure.'

Now therefore what appears from such a description of the saints in Holy Writ? A little flock; a small company united in one Spirit, but quite separate from the spirit that is in the world; a people of one mind, sons of God, in the midst of a crooked and perverse nation; blameless and harmless, though blamed and harmed; resolute and gentle, despite adversaries and persecutors. The church was as a pool of light in a sea of darkness: what consolation could there be for such a poor and meek people? What comfort to so tiny a beleaguered remnant? Why, precisely the same comfort as that ministered to the apostle.

This was the unique comfort inwardly ministered to all embracing the same gospel, to every one who had become 'partakers of my grace'. This same comfort provided the only consolation existent in a dark, alien, and hostile world of adversity for the poor pilgrims and strangers, God's people on earth. Yes, but, though inward, what consolation! Though spiritual, what comfort! Though interior, what fellowship!

'If there be therefore any consolation in Christ, if any comfort of love, if any fellowship of the Spirit, if any bowels and mercies, fulfil ye my joy, that ye be likeminded, having the same love, being of one accord, of one mind', Phil. 2:1,2. No strife; no vainglory; only lowliness of mind in which each esteemed other better than themselves.

No thought for what was one's own: thought only for what pertained to others. What likemindedness appeared! What being of one mind! But from whence came such lowliness of mind as this? Whence? From Christ Jesus. 'Let this mind be in you, which was also in Christ Jesus', Phil. 2:5.

In order to illustrate the sevenfold—perfect—lowliness of mind which was in Christ Jesus, the apostle commences by stating what was proper to Christ in and of himself: what ought to be predicated of him: what he himself thought, yea, what all deity revealed to be his proper estate and everlasting subsistence: 'Being in the form of God, he thought it not robbery to be equal with God', Phil. 2:6.

This passage is not brought in by the apostle to reveal divine mysteries: it is brought in to illustrate lowliness of mind. This single fact shows how divine mysteries were taken as the unquestioned basis of the faith, and as the ground of appeal for life, and to it, on the part of the faithful.

If the apostle speaks of the Son as being in the form of God, yet elsewhere writes distinctly of the Person of the Father, and that of the Spirit, as in that same form, it follows that a mystery is revealed.

This is the mystery of godliness: God is one in the indivisibility of his divine essence; yet, in a mystery, in the unity of that one divine essence there subsist three divine Persons. Mysteries are not understood: they are believed. And what Paul is saying here is that the Son thought—it is a question of

49

his mind: of his divine mentality—he thought in the unity of the deity that it was not robbery to own his equality in the one divine essence that was, is, and ever shall be, God: Father, Son, and Holy Ghost.

From this everlasting verity, he who was with God, and was God, John 1:1, who was in his own Person, as Son, eternally one with the Person of the Father, and with the Person of the Spirit—so that from eternity there subsisted three divine Persons in that one divine essence which is God—we see revealed a mystery unfathomable, the mystery of God, and of the faith.

I say, from this everlasting verity, the apostle now commences to show, from the mind that was in Christ Jesus, the sevenfold downward steps of humiliation on the part of the Son, according to a kind of lowliness that to mankind lies beyond all credibility to perceive in the deity.

But to those who are of faith, this mystery of God, and of the Father, and of Christ, is not and never can be a matter of understanding: it is a question of believing. And because we have received what we believe, it is the cause of our falling down prostrate with awe in unending worship at the revealed mystery of the mind that was in Christ Jesus, the mind of love divine, the mind of the deity.

First, out of the mystery of deity, and from unfathomable and everlasting divine relationships, the Son made himself of no reputation. Who can conceive of such a thing, of such a mind?

No one; no one, because the mystery of godliness, the nature of divine relationships, the subsistence of Father, Son, and Holy Ghost, as distinct divine Persons, eternally in those relationships, yet one in divine essence, one God, blessed for evermore, from everlasting to everlasting, these are all things utterly, infinitely, absolutely, and wholly beyond man's understanding.

These are things passing the capacity of all rational faculties, outside of all human ability to grasp even the dimensions without which it is impossible to begin the process of apprehension. Yes; but for all that it is not beyond the experience of revelation; not beyond the believing of faith; not beyond interior union and communion; not beyond shielding the eyes, prostrating the body, and worshipping, 'Holy, Holy, Holy, Lord God Almighty'.

See how *this* gospel genders reverence, that *sine qua non* of worship. Reverence not now at God's ineffable greatness. Now at his—*his!*—unspeakable stoop in lowliness. His mind. The mind that was in Christ Jesus. For he, in the form of God from everlasting, equal in deity from eternity, made himself—*he made himself*: he did it; of himself he did it—of no reputation.

'He emptied himself'. He made himself void of all that showed, all that outwardly manifested, who it was that had done this thing: one could not tell. Not from appearances. Appearances were voided. He emptied himself in relation to appearances. That was the first stage of the revelation of the mind that was in Christ Jesus, here set before mere brethren to emulate! 'Let *this* mind be in *you*.'

Having done this—*this!*—next 'He took upon him the form of a servant.' He did this, who was equal with God. If so, he did this, who was a distinct Person in deity. Then it must follow, Son of the Father from eternity, I Jn. 1:2. Here is a truth no Jew, no Sabellian, no Arian, no Taylorite—no lapsed ex Taylor brother absorbed into evangelicalism but, undetected, holding the same heresy—I say, here is a truth that none of these can think possible. For the basis of their rationalisation is that since a son cannot be equal with the father, then such a divine relationship cannot be eternal.

The Jews however, did not suffer from such carnal delusions: *they* knew what equality meant. 'He said that God was his

Father, making himself *equal* with God', Jn. 5:18. They would stone him for blasphemy, for they perceived clearly the inescapable connection of the relationship of the Father and the Son *once predicated of the deity*: it *must* be eternal. 'Because that thou, being a man, makest thyself *equal* with God', Jn. 10:33.

But he *was* equal with God. He did not *make* himself equal with God. *Being* equal with God—that is, though distinct in *Person*, ever one in *essence* with both the Father, and the Spirit. Nevertheless, it was *he* who made himself of no reputation—*one could no longer see by appearances who he was*.

Equal with God, Yes. But having made himself of no reputation he stooped again, once more, lower yet, 'And took upon him the form of a servant'. He was not a servant: he was God over all, blessed for evermore. But he had made himself of no reputation, so that then—*then*—he could assume servitude. I say, he was not a servant: but he appeared in the *form* of one. It was this that was in his mind. Nothing to show; nothing to tell; nothing to declare; no origin to record. A servant without reputation.

And mark this: the record of the humiliation and descent of the Son has not yet come to the incarnation. The text does not yet speak of his being made flesh. What has so far been revealed, twofold, is the mind that was in Christ Jesus *before* the incarnation. This is the second step in the mind that is set before brethren—*brethren*—to emulate. That is, he took upon him—having emptied himself—the form of a servant, to fulfil his service to God and the Father, in order that he *might* be made of the seed of David according to the flesh.

Hence thirdly, and not until thirdly, we come to the incarnation. Before the incarnation it is said, 'He cometh into the world', Heb. 10:5. Coming, he declares, 'A body hast thou prepared me'. If 'coming' into the world to that which was 'prepared' for him against that coming, then this declaration was made between heaven and earth, deity and humanity, before as yet he 'became flesh'.

The first two steps were in his mind and he took them. This third step also was in his mind, but with this difference: it entailed what was done for him—that is, the Father and the Spirit's preparation of a body—as well as his taking it upon himself. Thus 'He was made'—not made himself—'in the likeness of men.' The body was prepared for him. But one could not tell. One could observe 'the likeness of men'. But one would never have known who it was, or what had preceded, merely from the observation of that likeness.

Why not? Because of the steps in lowliness which had preceded. That is, because of what he had done already to hide from the creature *who* it was that was thus made flesh; to obscure from natural sight *who* it was that had become incarnate; to shield from carnal gaze *who* it was that disdained not the tiny seed of the woman. Thus *he* lay nine months in the womb of the virgin. This is to veil *who* it was that 'was made in the likeness of men'.

He was 'Made' in the likeness of men. Passivity is implied: the words indicate what was done for him, in order that this might be done by him. That is, the over-shadowing of the Father; the operation of the Holy Ghost; and the assumption of the Son of God.

This assumption of humanity took place at the moment of conception by the Holy Ghost of the seed of Mary. Then, precisely, the Son was 'made in the likeness of men'. Hence at the very outset of the incarnation it was said to Mary by the angel 'Therefore also that holy thing which shall be born of thee shall be called, The Son of God.'

Next, and fourthly, 'He was found in fashion as a man', Philippians 2:8. He who was in the form of God, who thought it not robbery to be equal with God, was found *in fashion as a man*? Yes, because he had 'emptied himself' of all that unapproachable light, that inconceivable glory, that ineffable radiance, proper to his divine nature, whilst, withal, retaining that nature in its full and perfect integrity.

But 'making himself of no reputation', there was no longer the *manifestation* of all that pertained to his intrinsic deity. The divine effulgence, eternal power, the everlasting glory that outshone from the divine nature were laid aside. The nature was the same. It was the hiding of its suited radiance, its innate glory, its unapproachable light, that marked the emptying.

Hence, incarnate, he could be among men, in their likeness, yet they 'knew him not'. 'He was in the world, and the world was made by him, but the world knew him not.' No, not by nature, not by appearance. Had there been the outward manifestation of Sonship, the divine outshining, yes.

But he to whom the manifestation belonged, to whom the outshining was proper, had emptied himself of all, made himself of no reputation. Who was he? To men, just another man, however unusual. He was found in fashion as a man. 'And the world knew him not.' Nor does it to this day. Indeed, even less is his invisible, spiritual presence, here now, known among us, or felt, or recognised as existing for what it is in reality.

Fifthly, in his wondrous, lowly, meek humanity, 'He humbled himself'. He served men, touched lepers, answered cries, washed feet, broke bread, denied none, ministered to all, sought not his own will, spake not his own words, went not at his own bidding, did nothing of himself. He spat and cried; he sighed and wept; he groaned and was troubled; he made strong supplication with tears; he was tempted in all points like as we are, yet without sin.

He was touched with the feeling of our infirmity: He was hungry and thirsty; hot and cold; tired and weary; he was among us as one that serveth. Matthew, Mark, Luke, and John testify with like awesome restraint of that humility which is beyond peer. For as one they witnessed, passing all understanding, the truth of his words: 'I am meek', saith he, 'and lowly of heart'.

He humbled himself. As if it were not enough that being who he was, and descending from whence he came, not enough, that he should be found in fashion as a man. No, not enough that he who came out of deity should be found in fashion as a man; not enough that he should be found on earth who came from the heavenly glory; not enough that he should be found in time who came from eternity; no, to him, it is not as though that were enough: for now, in that humiliation, yet further, yet lower, he 'humbled himself'.

That is, in manhood, on earth, in time, before men, as a servant to men, as man he humbled himself. How low? How far down? 'And became obedient unto death.' That is the sixth step of descent.

He was made a little lower than the angels for the suffering of death. That was what was in view. What law required this? No law ordained by angels. No law given to men. No law on earth. No commandment from Moses. No rule of righteousness for man. This was the divine nature, yet in all humanity; love divine, yet in all manliness; almighty power, yet in all weakness.

This utterly transcended the law of God given by angels in the hand of Moses as a rule of righteousness for men. This life of Christ Jesus, this mind, this unique life, this life of self-concealed deity in lowly manhood soared as high as the heavens are above the earth, and yet, paradoxically, this transcending height, this soaring ascendency, was in the lowliest, weakest, most pitiful humiliation of descent.

Obedient unto death? What does the law know of this? The law requires obedience for life. 'This do, and thou shalt live.' But grace was obedient unto death: 'This do, and thou shalt die.' A thing no law envisaged, and no legal commandment could require. But grace could desire it, and faith could answer to it, and by the faith of Jesus Christ he became obedient to the uttermost stoop, the ultimate price of love divine, even unto death.

Death for whom? Death for sinners. 'While we were yet sinners, Christ died for us', Rom. 5:8. 'Christ died for our sins according to the scriptures', I Cor. 15:3. Death for the ungodly: 'In due time Christ died for the ungodly', Rom. 5:6. Vicarious death. Substitutionary death. 'Who *his own self* bare *our* sins in *his own body* on the tree', I Peter 2:24. Obedient unto *that* death: 'By the obedience of one shall many be made righteous', Rom. 5:19.

That perfect depth, this sevenfold descent of humility, all that was in the mind of Christ Jesus, was reached in the nature of his death: '*Even* the death of the cross', Phil. 2:8. Why is this? Because of the humanly incomprehensible nature of the vicarious suffering which that sacrificial death entailed, far and away beyond the dreadful physical agonies of the crucifixion in and of itself.

The sufferings of the crucifixion were inflicted by men and stood in the most excruciating physical pain. But when the Holy Ghost speaks of the sufferings of Christ he speaks of sufferings inflicted by Almighty God, standing in absolutes, infinities, and eternities beyond the comprehension of mortal man.

Why? Because they were sufferings to offer atonement; sufferings to expiate sin; sufferings to appease wrath; sufferings to effect propitiation. They were sufferings which were endured in the place of sacrifice for the sin of the world, 'Behold the

Lamb of God, which taketh away the sin of the world'. Above all, they were sufferings for the sins of a multitude so great that they cannot be numbered: 'Christ was once offered to bear the sins of many', 'This is my blood of the new testament which is shed for many for the remission of sins.'

The sufferings of Christ Jesus rendered full satisfaction to God on behalf of all those for whom he died. That is, firstly, satisfaction to the curse and broken sanctions of the law, besides satisfaction to that law in and of itself. But, as if that were not enough to be poured out from heaven's fury, yet there remained the vengeance and wrath of Almighty God, according to his own divine nature, 'the vengeance of eternal fire'. This, secondly, was over, above, and infinitely beyond all that just punishment due to the broken rule of righteousness for men prescribed in the law of Moses.

Transcending all, Christ's sufferings satisfied the very right-eousness of God in and of himself, the righteousness of his own intrinsic divine nature. It is *that* which men have outraged, beyond all earthly rules, and it is *that* for which God both takes vengeance and exacts just punishment. For *that* Christ suffered vicariously in death, bringing in 'the righteousness of God by faith of Jesus Christ', Rom. 3:22.

The substitutionary sacrifice of Christ was offered up upon the cross not only to requite the righteousness of the law but also to satisfy divine righteousness.

Under the law God was seen to be righteous as a Judge by his just judgments in punishing the transgressions of men against the commandments. But under the gospel what has come to light is the righteousness of God within himself irrespective of his judging according to the rule of righteousness for men.

The gospel therefore reveals the righteousness of the deity, as such. Not as called forth to judge *men* according to the rule delivered to *them*; but as it is intrinsically, within the deity, being proper to the divine nature in and of itself. By Christ's satisfaction to this divine righteousness, to the very righteousness of God in himself, the redeemed have been brought through the rent veil to God in his own Person.

This is the righteousness—the everlasting righteousness—of God interior to himself. This is that righteousness of the deity, measured from the infinite heights of divine glory to the lowest depths of fallen humanity, thence to gauge the equivalent of eternal punishment to be borne by Christ Jesus, the sin-bearer, for us men and for our salvation.

Through such unimaginable floods of God's wrath Christ waded, till the waters came into his very soul; till all God's waves and billows of everlasting wrath broke over him; till he sank in deep mire, wherein was no standing, beneath great depths and under incomprehensible sufferings.

Thus he requited the righteousness of God against the sins and iniquities of his people, rendering to divine justice a satisfaction, through his broken body and shed blood on their behalf, equal to all that they had incurred in judgment against themselves from the divine nature for eternity.

That is, in the death of the cross Christ paid in suffering the equivalent punishment of all those for whom he died, afterwards to be brought to saving faith. This accomplished redemption was sealed with shed blood; settled in a broken body; confirmed through sufferings unto death; and ratified by vicarious atonement.

It is this that reveals the mind that was in Christ Jesus, who went beneath all—even so far as the death of the cross—that he might bring his people over all, thence to the everlasting glory of an eternal inheritance.

With such glory in mind, Paul writes to the Philippians; and, moreover, through that epistle, writes to us all: 'Let this mind be in *you*, which was in Christ Jesus.'

'This mind, which in Christ Jesus was,
　　let also in you be:
who, being in the form of God,
　　abode in deity;

No robbery he did it think,
　　no taking from his name,
that he himself as one with God
　　equality should claim.

But of no reputation he
　　himself spared not to make,
for of a servant he the form
　　upon himself did take;

And in the likeness of mankind
　　he made was to appear:
and being in man's fashion found,
　　he unto men drew near.

Himself he humbled, yea, and though
　　of all he suffered loss,
to death became obedient,
　　the death e'en of the cross.

Wherefore God also highly hath
　　exalted him in love,
and given him a name which is
　　all other names above:

That every knee be made to bow
　　at Jesus' holy name,
of things in heaven, and in earth,
　　and underneath the same;

And every tongue confess aloud
　　that Jesus Christ is Lord,
to God the Father glory that
　　all creatures might afford.'

THE CONTENT OF PHILIPPIANS

Part Two
Philippians Ch. 2:12 to Ch. 3:2

'Be ye followers together of me', Phil. 3:17

IN verses 12 to 16 of Chapter 2 Paul exhorts those whom he terms—and terms from the heart—'my beloved', that they should continue in obedience to work out their own salvation with fear and trembling, because it is God that worketh in them to will and to do of his good pleasure. That is, the very same volitions and earnest intentions which they themselves feel as Paul's obedient spiritual children, really have their origins from the hidden inworking of Almighty God.

However this exhortation, verse 12, commences with the word 'Wherefore', implying that a premise had been laid down on the basis of which this exhortation to outwork salvation follows. As if to say, This doctrine is true, 'Wherefore', that exhortation follows.

Which doctrine is true? What premise follows? Why, the doctrine that a certain mind was in Christ Jesus. Notwithstanding that he was in the form of God, that he thought it not robbery to be equal with God, yet this mentality of unique humility and peerless self-sacrifice was in him. This took him down into death, yea, into the lower parts of the earth, in the meekest submission to the will of God.

So pleasing was this for God to behold in his beloved Son, that, raising him from the dead, bursting asunder the gates of death, sweeping aside the power of the grave, carrying him above all heavens, God highly exalted him. God has exalted him beyond all comprehension, so that not only is he Lord of all, but every knee shall be made to bow in submission, and every tongue shall be made to confess in subjection, whether friend or foe, devil or angel, sheep or goat.

In that great day of righteous recompence and just vengeance, every creature shall bow and confess the Lord of glory, before being sent to their place for eternity. Mark that, it is certain to come: every single creature, no matter their destiny, shall bow the knee and confess with the tongue the majesty, honour, and power of the Lord Jesus Christ on the throne of his glory.

Now, so to follow Christ in his humiliation; so to be as he was in the world; so to walk as we have him for an example; so to let this mind be in us which was in Christ Jesus; more: so to bow the knee continually in this present world and on earth; so to confess him before men throughout our remaining lifetime; that is, to do voluntarily throughout this present life, what all must do perforce at the end of it, this is to outwork salvation with a witness.

'Let this mind be in you, which was in Christ Jesus.' Here is no 'law as a rule of life'. No law ever given could have justly demanded or remotely required the depth of this humility. This is Christ as our life. 'Wherefore' what was true of his mentality, his mind, is to be outworked by the inworking of God, in all the brethren: 'For we have the mind of Christ.'

Whence it is to be observed that the whole doctrinal premise
—'Wherefore'—of this remarkable and distinguished exhortation of the apostle Paul to the saints at Philippi lies in the truth
of what Christ did for God, and for what in consequence
God has done for Christ. That is the rule of life: to be fulfilled
in our life and mentality with the lowliness of mind characteristic of every step in the life of the Redeemer.

'God hath highly exalted him', verse 9. Now, *that* is the
resurrection, after such a sevenfold stoop, such a humiliating
pathway, such a descent into death, on the part of the Saviour
and on the behalf of his people. I say, *that* is the resurrection in
Christ, the resurrection of the just, the resurrection to everlasting glory, to an eternal inheritance, the resurrection to
the world to come whereof we speak.

There are things not to be missed in this remarkable exhortation, noticeable by their absence from contemporary
Christendom. For example, the apostolic authority and the
saints' submission.

First, the apostolic authority. The apostle was sent 'for
obedience to the faith among all nations, for his name', Rom.
1:5, and again Rom. 15:18, 'to *make* the Gentiles *obedient*, by
word and deed', hence, Rom. 6:17, 'Ye have *obeyed* from the
heart that form of doctrine which was delivered you'. And, of
course, in this place, Phil. 2:12, 'Wherefore, my beloved, as *ye
have always obeyed*, not as in my presence only, but now much
more in my absence.'

The apostles spake not their own word, did not their own
will, died daily, lived by the faith of the Son of God, preached
not themselves but Christ Jesus as Lord, Christ himself being
mighty in them by the power of the Holy Ghost. And if these
things be so of the apostolate, and of that holy ministry subject
to the apostles, whose calling was confirmed by their word,

then, Who among us today would not wish to be obedient, that is, much more in the apostles' absence, since their word alone provides us with the only inviolate, infallible, and certain direction in salvation?

Neither are these things obsolete, as though they passed away with the apostolic age. Otherwise where would we be, but utterly forsaken of God, and given up before we had so much as drawn breath? But 'Lo, I am with you alway, even unto the end of the age', Mt. 28:20, and again, Heb. 13:8 'Jesus Christ the same yesterday, and today, and for ever.' Then, as unchanging as is the Lord, so also are his ways. These things are not made obsolete with the passing of the apostles: though they honour and require subjection to those apostles.

Thus both the apostolic authority and the saints' submission are the same yesterday, today, and for ever, preserved in that apostolic ministry sent from the Son of God in heaven till the end of the age, and maintained in the saints gathered under that ministry and subject to its authority till the end of time.

Hence the apostle's association of Timothy with him in the joint authorship ascribed to the epistle. Though the writer was the apostle, and the disciple his son in the gospel, yet they are portrayed as one: 'Paul and Timotheus', Phil. 1:1.

This principle is even more apparent in the pastoral epistles, namely, I and II Timothy and Titus. From distant countries Paul directs the ministry in the absence of the apostleship, vesting in the sent and subject ministry of such as Timothy and Titus the authority—the sole authority—not only to continue and preserve the apostolic doctrine, fellowship, discipline, and ordinances, but to ordain elders, bishops, deacons. Moreover to mark out those called in their turn and place to the same work.

In the pastoral epistles the things to which the ministry sent from Christ must be strictly submissive are carefully written down. This serves two purposes: there can be no doubt of the duty of called ministers, and there can be no question of what the saints should—and must—expect from them. This known, written, and recorded duty cuts off the opportunity of false teachers remaining undetected, and it preserves the brethren of later ages—even to our own—from having the least possibility of being deceived. But what has happened? Generally, these particular pastoral apostolic writings have been either wrested, or treated with indifferent contempt.

This indisputable fact exposes the defiance of Plymouth Brethren teaching, which denies Christ's rights in both the ordination and the office of minister in its first principle. This system is guilty of overturning the scriptures written for the very purpose which it denies, particularly I and II Timothy and Titus. It terminates the apostolic ministry immediately after the death of the apostles and those appointed by them, reducing Timothy and Titus to the invented term 'delegates'.

Nothing could be more destructive of Christ's authority. However, the followers of J.N. Darby and the Plymouth Brethren justify this destructive razing of Zion's foundations by pointing to the errors of denominationalism and clerisy. Concerning what was wrong they may very well have been right: but—bolstered by their censorious correctness in judging the faults of others—what is this that they have substituted in the place of what they have ruined?

What? In the place of ruin they have put anarchy. The ruin of what? Of the continuity of Christ in sending the apostolic ministry, and of the requirement of that ministry to be faithful to Christ and his apostles by subject obedience and enforcement of the doctrine, discipline, and ordinance, laid down till the end of time in the epistles I and II Timothy and Titus.

So how dare these Brethren appoint themselves elders? According to the apostle only ordained ministers can appoint elders. However, denying the scripture its authority, and Christ his rights, they appoint themselves instead. Thus they cast out the ministry properly so-called, and put themselves in the seat they have just overthrown. Hence they rob the pastoral epistles of any force by denying the continuation of the office of those persons to whom alone what they usurp belongs.

Oh, yes, and they fill to overflowing the void they have thus made in scripture with the corruption of an ordinance not even mentioned in any one—much less in all three—of the pastoral epistles in question, putting *that*—as the papists put the Mass—instead of the central place of the preaching and teaching of the gospel by those sent to do so! Thus they destroy by a form the real means by which the saints are gathered and brought into divine unity, so to witness and function as one body according to the scriptures.

But the word of the Lord stands sure: 'How shall one preach except he be sent?' Sent? In place of Sending, Brethrenism substitutes Ruin, a system unscriptural, unevangelical, and anarchistic in its basic principle. This is at the root of Brethrenism. And neither the errors of Clericalism, nor the cherished mantra of the Brethren chanted against 'one-man ministry' —though charming never so wisely—can ever justify their heretical theory of Ruin by which they jettison the office of Minister and the scriptures written to govern that ministry.

Nor can it ever excuse this anarchistic and levelling system from its failure to return precisely to that order which was in the beginning. That is, to the apostolic authority on the one hand continued in the same subject ministry as Timothy and Titus; and to the saints' submission to that ministry on the other hand, both being sustained in the like humility. They will complain, 'But you cannot rebuild!' I answer, No: *but Christ can.* Only, your system disbelieves and prevents it by its avowed basis.

In contrast, how lovely it is to behold that order envisaged in Paul's beloved brethren, exhorted to lowly obedience, to do all things without murmurings and disputings, blameless and harmless, the sons of God without rebuke. And this amidst a crooked and perverse nation, a hostile world, a scene of adversity. But it is God that worketh in—that is, within—the saints, and, together, they are to work out their own salvation with fear and trembling.

How such trembling reverence has departed from the present generation. The fear of God is today conspicuous by its absence. Yet of the first saints it was written 'Great fear came upon all the church'. They feared, yes, and trembled. But where has all this gone? It has gone with the departure of the glory. It has long gone; and the people are hardened. Ichabod is over the whole generation: 'For the glory is departed.'

At the beginning, in the very atmosphere of eternity, with the felt presence of the living God, the saints trembled together under the mighty power of the salvation of God: it is not, 'Work out *thine* own salvation'. It is 'Work out *your* own salvation'.

Here was one people, in the fear of God, separated from the world, indwelt by Father, Son, and Holy Ghost, outworking salvation in one body, so that, holding forth the word of life, they shone as lights in the darkness of this world. Enduring to the end. So the apostle would rejoice in the day of Christ, that he had not run in vain, neither laboured in vain:

'Beloved, as ye always have
　　obeyed me heretofore,
not only when I present am,
　　but in my absence more,

Work ye your own salvation out,
　　as is both meet and due,
with fear and trembling evident
　　in every one of you.

Because that it is God which doth
    work in you inwardly,
that thereby of his pleasure good
    both will and do might ye.

Do all things without murmurings,
    disputings, or discord:
that wholly blameless ye may be,
    the harmless sons of God;

Those 'gainst whom there is no rebuke,
    although ye should be found
amidst a crooked nation where
    perverseness doth abound;

Among whom also in the world
    as lights ye shine abroad,
as one together holding forth
    of life the very word.'

Next Paul declares his readiness to be 'offered up', as if on an altar. That is, since his imprisonment and trial were from no cause other than persecution for his preaching the gospel, it would be upon the altar of that preaching having been made effectual to the Gentiles that he would be offered: a willing and thankful victim 'Offered upon the sacrifice and service of your faith'.

Since that faith came to them by the pure, only, and true gospel of the grace of Christ preached by Paul, he adds the explanation: 'If', he writes, he should be sacrificed on such an altar, 'I joy, and rejoice with you all'. Then let them not mourn, but joy and rejoice with him.

They were not to despair as though all were lost: all was gained. There was nothing in this life but Christ, whom they had gained by the very gospel which provided the occasion for Paul's sacrifice. And, as to that sacrifice, 'to die is gain'.

Following this, Paul speaks of his purposing to send Timoth-eus, but not before he knew how it would go with him at the trial. As to Timothy, as a son with the father he had served with Paul in the gospel, and this had been proven over long years of experience.

There was no other minister left to Paul of like mind. Phil. 2:20, 'For I have no man likeminded, who will naturally care for your state.' And if that were true *then*, what can one expect *now*? I expect Christ in his great faithfulness still to send if it be but one or two likeminded sons to the apostle, till the last day; sons, that is, who will, on the one hand, 'naturally care for your state', and, on the other, willingly be 'offered up upon the sacrifice and service of your faith'.

Now appears a most revealing statement, Phil. 2:21, 'For all seek their own, not the things which are Jesus Christ's.' Do remember the era in which this was written: that is, during the lifetime of the apostles. And, realizing, ask yourself whether you think to escape controversy, affliction, declension, apathy, division, complacency, apostasy, a great falling away, a famine of the word of God, an absence of sent ministers, yes, and persecution, enmity, adversity, suffering, trial, and even death, in such a latter day as this?

Ask yourself what does this expression mean 'All seek their own', an expression that must in the nature of things be vastly compounded as time passes, so that beyond measure today, 'All seek their own, not the things which are Jesus Christ's'?

And mark this: it was not that they did not *profess* Jesus Christ. It was that *whilst* professing him, they couldn't care less about his things, because they were entirely occupied with their own: 'All seek their own.'

This is to be a foolish builder; a goat and not a sheep. This is to be seed sown on bad ground. This is to be a foolish virgin.

This is to lay up for oneself the words at the last judgment: 'Depart from me: I never knew you.'

But then, what *are* the things of Jesus Christ which no man in those countries save Paul and Timotheus sought in the ministry, since 'all'— *all*—'seek their own', using *his* things as a means of gaining *theirs?* Yes, but, precisely what constitutes 'the things which are Jesus Christ's'?

Well, for example: The old testament. It is his: it is only lent to us. The new testament. It is not our property, or scholars' property: it is one of his things. The holy bible.

The Greek text owned of him from the beginning, and, in principle, recovered at the Reformation, called The *Textus Receptus.* Likewise the English translation owned of God for centuries: the Authorized Version, largely taken from the martyr Tyndale's much earlier translation, bought for us today at the price of his being strangled and burned at the stake.

The entire gospel, in every part, and the sum of the parts: all this—every part of it—is Jesus Christ's, and no one else's. No thief has the right to subtract from it; no ripper to lacerate it; no heretic to divide it; no Arminian to multiply it; no legalist to add to it: it is *his.* And his *as it is.*

This evangel declares his Person, his one Person, his divine Person; his Sonship, his eternal Sonship; his incarnation, his humanity; his having both divine and human natures in union without confusion in one Person; his body, his blood; his perfection, his spirituality; his immensity, his humility: in a word, the mystery that is Christ. It is his: his to reveal, his to obscure; his to give, his to withhold. Sovereignly, imperatively, absolutely, in his own prerogative, all is his.

His life is his: from eternity; throughout the old testament; within the new testament; in glory; to eternity. The work of

Christ is his: his birth; his baptism; his transfiguration; his visitation; his death; his resurrection; his ascension. His ministry is his: his Galilean ministry; his ministry on the way; his Jerusalem ministry; his ministry from the glory.

His divine administration is his: the ministration of justification; of life; of reconciliation; of the word; of the Spirit; of the new testament; and of the glory. All these things are his, his to give, his to withhold. None can claim them: he can bestow them. But they are his absolutely. No one has a *right* to what is his.

The ministry is his: whether of the Spirit in the body, which is one thing; or whether from the Head to the body, which is another thing. These things are Christ's. They do not belong to colleges, or principals, or tutors. They are *his*. And his to send directly to the people, fully prepared, from the heavenly glory, and by the indwelling Spirit.

The church—the *ecclesia*—is his. It is not man's: it is not for man to take over, divide, reorganize, or copy in various denominations as though each separate division were the church. It is not for man to manage, appoint, elect, or set up in rivalry the one division against the other—indeed there is no justification for the existence of *any* other than *his own* church.

Those churches that are of man; or those sects, denominations or apostasies which they invent; or halls, societies, or congregations which they set up: all of them, not being *his*, should be shut down immediately. It is a fearful compound of robbery, presumption, and arrogance. The nature, administration, and gathering of the church should be left in faith to him whose right it is to be the one Head of one body. After all, what would *you* think if you came out of anaesthetic with a dozen more heads from other men grafted on as many dismembered parts of other creatures onto *your* divided body?

The ordinances are his, and his to ordain. It is not for the Queen, or for the Prime Minister, or for some advisory body, much less for foreigners from Rome, nor yet the church membership, neither the Brethren hall, to ordain bishops, or elect deacons, or raise up elders: this is *his* sole right, and he alone can perform it. Order is his. Prayer is his. Baptism is his. The Supper is his.

The psalms are his; the spiritual songs are his; the hymns of the new testament are his; all being called 'The word of Christ' in song. These things are not ours, either for poets or would-be hymn writers to invent, they are his to convey. Nor ought we to sing *anything* but what he bestows and commands.

Likewise with worship. It is his: he must lead it, and lead it by his own Spirit. Worship is in Spirit and truth; it is in sonship; it is to the Father; and Christ leads it: these are his things. There is no place for man here; no place for the flesh. God cannot away with what is of man or the flesh. Only what is of Christ is acceptable with God. Time fails to tell of Christ's things! The inheritance is his, the hope, the resurrection, the glory, and the world to come. All things are Christ's.

I confess to you, I love, love, love these things. His things. I love them, and love every one of them, and I love him, so much, I cannot hold my peace: let them cast me out if they will. God knoweth, my conscience bears me witness, I live for his things, I cannot tolerate man taking over any one of them: no, not the least of them. I live for them, and by grace, by my God, I would die for them.

These are the things which are Jesus Christ's; which in Paul's day, no man sought after, 'For all seek their own, not the things which are Jesus Christ's.' And do you think, in the very nature of things, it is any better now? Or does not your own conscience tell you, Rather, it is far worse now?

71

So Paul purposes to send Timothy, his own son in the gospel, who sought the things which are Jesus Christ's, and lived for them, likeminded with Paul. But before that he would send Epaphroditus, their messenger, and his brother and companion, who risked his life to fulfil their service and sacrifice to Paul. Now the apostle, in turn, hastens to restore this faithful servant of Christ to the Philippians.

Thus Paul comes to Philippians Chapter 3, evidently intending to conclude the epistle at this point, Phil. 3:1, 'Finally, my brethren'. But it is far from finally, and thankful all saints should be for the long digression—a kind of parenthesis—because in fact it is not until into Chapter 4 that the apostle returns to his originally intended conclusion, repeating the words 'Finally, brethren', Phil. 4:8. But what made him digress?

He had said, Phil. 3:1, 'Finally, my brethren, rejoice in the Lord.' Did he digress to expound on the subject of rejoicing? No, not upon that. But so often he exhorted to joy and rejoicing, it was indeed a repetition, hence he says 'to write the same'—for he knows he is repeating himself—'to write the same things to me indeed is not grievous.' This is no more than an explanation of his repeated exhortation to rejoice.

Then what makes him digress after 'finally' in 3:1, throughout Chapter 3, continuing beyond into the first seven verses of Chapter 4, before returning to the words, 'Finally, brethren', Phil. 4:8?

What? It is a digression springing entirely from the last, closing, phrase in 3:1, 'For you it is safe'. It was their *safety*. *That* moved his heart, stirred his bowels, flashed with divine light in his mind: their *safety*. Now, safety is *salvation*. It is at this point that the extended digression occurs.

Safety is from *danger*. Salvation is out of the hand of *enemies*. But fools make a mock of danger. The simple trust enemies.

Here, Paul would have them to be wise: to know their enemies: to be *safe*. Hence he proceeds to warn them immediately, Ch. 3:2.

'*Beware*'. There can be no word more closely associated with *the warning of what is unsafe*. For their safety, therefore, the apostle proceeds to describe exactly of whom to beware. Said the Lord Jesus 'Beware of men'. Saith Paul, 'Beware of dogs, beware of evil workers, beware of the concision', Phil. 3:2. You see how plainly Paul speaks, and under what strong characterization he describes the enemies of the saints and of the gospel, without deliverance from whom they could not be saved.

And are we so safe today, that it is all right that we are kept even from hearing such plainness of speech, and denied on every hand such clearness of warning? No, we are not so safe: we are in more danger today, than were the Philippians in their day. Then why does nobody warn us with equal, if not more vehement, force?

Why? Because the enemies of whom Paul warned the Philippians have now filled the churches, denominations, and halls, so as to control them, and hence they are hardly likely to warn us against themselves. And if it be not so, Why do we hear no warnings?

For Paul warns of dogs, evil workers, and the concision, *in* the church, not out of it. In the then undivided church, not the present divided and denominated one. If so, *how much more* ought we to be warned for our safety, and, at that, without any mealy-mouthed mumbling, mincing of words, or beating about the bush? But platitudes and affected 'niceness' are all that we get, leaving us without a clue either of the danger, the urgency, the antidote, or the way of safety.

But we trust in God, that you may find us without dissimulation, and faithful followers of Paul in the holy word of God, subject to the immense authority of the apostles, and caring for your priceless safety. Thus we shall speak to you the word of truth, the gospel of your salvation, with all boldness, come what may. Hence we proceed to show you not only the meaning of the apostle, and those of whom he warns the Philippians, but the meaning to us, and of whom he cautions us also.

First the apostle warns us of dogs. But what does he mean by 'dogs'? One of three things: either literal dogs; or those worldly men who so act like dogs that he calls them by that name; or else religious dogs of the same nature in the church. Since the threefold warning goes on to speak of what undoubtedly refers to religious men, we may safely conclude that he bids us beware of religious dogs.

Well, from the contemporary dissolution of all plain speaking into characterless sentiment, you would think that Paul's 'dogs' are an ancient canine species which became quite extinct no sooner than described. Is that so? Let us see.

The 22nd Psalm is famous for its prophetic vision and pinpoint accuracy over the events of the crucifixion of Christ some nine hundred years before Jesus either came into the world, or was, at the last, nailed to the cross. 'They part my garments among them, and cast lots upon my vesture', cried David in a prophetic trance.

Nearly a whole millennium later John the apostle, who saw the crucifixion from beginning to end—and you know that his witness is true—told of this very event, which took place before his eyes, 'They parted my raiment among them, and for my vesture they cast lots. These things therefore the soldiers did', John 19:24.

David saw in vision centuries beforehand that which made him cry out—not knowing what he said, nor why he said it—being full of the Holy Ghost, 'They pierced my hands and my feet'! But they did not. No one pierced David's hands and feet. But, saith Peter on the Day of Pentecost, 'David, being a prophet', 'seeing this before', 'spake of Christ.'

Nine hundred years after David spake of Christ, Christ came. But they hung the Saviour on a tree, in the process of which they nailed him through his hands and his feet. This was called Crucifixion, in which, even as David foresaw, they pierced Christ's hands and feet.

And as if this were not testimony enough, Jesus, risen from the dead, rebukes to this day the blind unbelief of man in Thomas, who had said, 'Except I shall see in his hands the print of the nails, and put my finger into the print of the nails, and thrust my hand into his side, I will not believe.' Came Jesus, risen from the dead, and said, 'Reach hither thy finger, and behold my hands; and reach hither thy hand, and thrust it into my side: and be not faithless, but believing', Jn. 20:27.

'Be not faithless'? Why faithless? Because of unbelief: 'O fools, and slow of heart to believe all that the prophets have spoken.' Near a thousand years before it happened, David prophetically described in detail *exactly* what was to take place a thousand years later. And yet, is even *that* any more remarkable than the demonstrable proof shown to Thomas by Jesus after he had risen from the dead?

Case after case might be multiplied from Psalm 22 of what would be absolutely incredible except for two things: First, the omniscience of God, by whom David saw forward into the yawning future, prophesying what would happen nine hundred years before each detail unfolded moment by moment when the time was fulfilled. Second, the unshakeable reliability of the scriptures: 'O fools' said Jesus, 'and slow of heart to believe *all* that the prophets have spoken.' This rebuke was delivered to the disciples after Jesus was risen from the dead, with the marks verifying that death plain for all to see.

But what is all this to do with dogs? Psalm 22:16 states 'For dogs have compassed me: the assembly of the wicked have inclosed me: they pierced my hands and my feet.' But who compassed Jesus? Judas, one of the twelve. He led the assembly of the wicked which compassed Jesus about at Gethsemane. He led them to the palace of the high priest. Unlawfully Jesus was condemned by the chief priests. They haled him into their assembly. That assembly was called, The Sanhedrin.

The Sanhedrin was composed of the chief priests, elders, scribes, Pharisees, Sadducees, doctors, rulers of the people, with the whole hierarchy of the religious system. This was the assembly which compassed him about. None other.

True, they outmanoeuvred and trapped Pilate into commanding the soldiers actually to do the work of piercing Jesus' hands and feet. You say, Then it was Pilate. Or the soldiers. Peter the apostle says, 'Ye men of Israel, hear these words; Jesus of Nazareth *ye* have taken, and by wicked hands have crucified and slain', Acts 2:22,23.

Now, find the modern equivalent of the chief priests, elders, rulers of the people, the scribes, the Pharisees, the Sadducees, the doctors, the Herodians, the entire hierarchy of religious leaders, and you have found Peter's 'Ye', David's 'Assembly', and Paul's 'Dogs'.

If not, what *does* it mean, since—despite modern incredulity —this breed is not said to have become extinct, but rather to have increased so much the more till at the last they have filled and taken over the professing church, or, as scripture calls it, the 'outer court'. Beware of dogs.

Next Paul warns the brethren of 'evil workers'. These are the same as those elsewhere called 'workers of iniquity', and, of course, refers to the religious of this sort, not the worldly.

76

Do bear in mind the context, in which Paul intended to conclude this epistle 'finally', 3:1, by exhorting his brethren to rejoice in the Lord. This exhortation, however repetitive, was safe. That word, 'Safe', triggered the parenthetical digression with which we are now concerned. Safe? Then in the following verses he interrupts his once 'final' conclusion: Safety lies in the avoidance of dogs, evil workers, and the concision.

As we see here, at the centre of this dangerous triad lies those whom Paul calls 'evil workers' or 'workers of iniquity'. We know that they infiltrate and permeate the church—the *ecclesia*—we know that they are religious, but the question remains, What gives them their distinctive character among the three the avoidance of each of whom is essential to escape from deadly and everlasting danger?

Evil workers are those who do not, and will not, follow the apostolic ministry, and, to put it plainly, the apostolic minister, either in Paul himself, or in his son Timothy, or in those subsequently sent from the Head, Christ, in the heavenly glory. The ministers they defy are those who manifest their meek subjection and submission to Christ and his apostles in their doctrine, discipline, fellowship, ordinances, and authoritative insistence and enforcement of the same, to the end of the age.

Whoso claims apostolic authority, or ministry, or pastoral office, or gift, or place, yet fails to follow those in whom this example is manifest, there you find the evil worker. 'Brethren, be followers together of me, and *mark them* which walk, *so as ye have us*—plural: *us—for an ensample*', Phil. 3:17.

And how do you walk, Paul, Timothy, and those who follow your example, whom the brethren are to follow to this day, marking *your* walk in contrast to that of those evil workers who refuse to walk in your exemplary way, or to tread in your footsteps? 'For many walk, of whom I have told you often'—so that you see the apostle *never avoided the naming of persons or parties dangerous to the safety of the brethren, or of the church, no matter what controversy or hatred this stirred up against himself* —'many walk of whom I have told you often, and now tell you even weeping.'

Weeping, not for *them*, the evil workers, but for the havoc which they would work in God's assembly, the divisions they would cause in the one *ecclesia*, the church, and the multitudes who, blinded by their trickery, would increasingly wander out of the way of understanding, into the depth of destruction, by following these evil workers, elsewhere called 'blind leaders of the blind', whose end is to fall into the ditch of everlasting darkness.

What marked them out? Nothing too obvious. That is, unless one laid the apostolic walk against their walk, and the apostolic word against their word, and the apostles' fellowship against their fellowship, which soon showed how cross their path was to that of the apostolic ministry.

What was the evil of these 'evil workers'? Nothing too obvious. That is, unless one marked the righteousness which characterized the apostolic ministry, which soon made apparent the unrighteousness of these evil workers, who, under the guise of 'love' dissolved all righteousness into a liquid morass of adaptability to the flesh, the world, and an outward show of Christianity.

What marked out these evil workers? First, They are 'the enemies of the cross of Christ', Phil. 3:18. How was that? Because they did not preach the substitutionary atonement, namely, that Christ actually redeemed his people when he died; that of necessity he died for the sheep and not for the goats; and that he really and effectually purchased his people with his own blood when it was shed.

Hence, by his blood, at the cross, Christ brought in a divine righteousness which was reckoned or imputed to the account of his elect *then*, a righteousness exterior to themselves, in the bank of heaven, credited to their account *at the moment at which Christ died*, a righteousness which is said to be 'unto them'—Rom. 3:22—through the death of Christ. This righteousness is at the very heart of the gospel. To it sinners and the ungodly are called. When these believe, then that which was before 'unto them', is, at the moment of believing, 'upon them' Rom. 3:22.

God thus imputes righteousness, in their conscious knowledge of it, so that their faith now credits—in their own experience —what the blood of Christ *had* obtained for them, and what God *had* laid up for them, at the time at which Christ died. Now, however, *they* are aware of it, God conveys the knowledge of it to their own belief, and when he does this, believers are said to be justified by faith. This is a most wholesome doctrine, and very full of comfort.

But evil workers are the enemies of this doctrine. They hate it. Then, they are the enemies of the cross of Christ. They walk contrary to it. But Paul walked by it, and to this day calls you to follow his example by us who follow him, and mark those who walk contrary thereto, so as to beware of them.

Well, try out this rule for yourselves, for we can do nothing against the truth, but only for it. Therefore we have declared to you plainly that they are enemies of the cross of Christ who do not distinctly, clearly, and continuously preach and walk by this doctrine, though such deviates fill the pulpits, halls, and churches the length and breadth of Great Britain.

And of this truth our own Articles tell us, namely, 'That we are justified by faith only is a most wholesome doctrine, and very full of comfort', Article XI of the Thirty-nine Articles of the Church of England. This Article on Justification is true. But justification rests on atonement. And atonement was wrought for all the elect at the cross of Christ.

Whoso preaches otherwise, or walks otherwise, or fails to preach this continually, Paul designates an 'evil worker', because they are 'enemies of the cross of Christ'. Hence the apostle warns you to avoid such, as you would avoid an injection of anthrax, AIDS, and the bubonic plague all mixed up in the same syringe, about to be plunged into your life-blood.

'Whose end is destruction', Phil. 3:19. So was the end of those who contracted the black death. But the black death of those who follow the false teachers whom Paul designates as the enemies of the cross of Christ—who profess by beguiling words to hold the very thing of which they are enemies, though they never preach or walk by it as did Paul—I say, the black death of those who follow these deceivers is that of outer darkness and a bottomless pit. 'Whose end is destruction.'

They sentimentalize the crucifixion: but they rubbish justification. They depict Jesus on the cross: yet they vandalize substitutionary atonement. They can coo, croon, or rock their choruses, but they cannot teach, reason, or instruct on ransom, reconciliation, propitiation, expiation, oblation, redemption, remission, nor are the words substitutionary atonement in their mouths, and as to their hearts, with all their strength they detest and hate imputed righteousness and justification by faith only.

'Whose end is destruction', and, it follows, since they are blind leaders of the blind, all who follow them shall fall into the like ditch. But follow Paul. Follow the apostolic ministry. Follow Article XI. 'Be ye followers together of me', says the apostle. Well: there is his example, in both doctrine and walk, and what could be more plain, more illuminating, or more honestly set before you?

Paul comes to the next characteristic of these deadly invaders of the church: 'Whose God is their belly.' Now do not be deceived by the apparent simplicity of this statement. Not literally their belly. Not merely that they are gluttons. For, here, *the belly is envisaged as the seat of the appetites.*

Which appetites? Oh, any appetites. Such as greed; ambition; place-seeking; flattery; pride; snobbery; lust; uncleanness; enmity; hatred; emulation; strife; vain glory; covetousness: the 'belly' holds them all. And these enemies of the cross of Christ so pursued their appetites; so connived at lust to fulfil them; so lived for them, so winked at the same thing in others; that the life and vigour they put into *that* was precisely the life and vigour they *should* have put into *worship*.

Then, that *was* their worship. If so, their god was the self-gratification of those appetites. As saith the apostle Paul of these evil workers, the enemies of the cross of Christ, Phil. 3:19, 'whose God is their belly'.

Then, 'their glory is in their shame', Phil. 3:19. They glory in appearances, II Cor. 5:12; they glory in condemnation, II Cor. 3:9; they glory in men, I Thess. 2:6; they glory in vanity, Gal. 5:26; they glory in man's praise, Mt. 6:2; they glory in the flesh, Gal. 6:13: but they do not glory in the Lord, I Cor. 1:31, and hence they come short of the glory of God, Rom. 3:23, having their part with the hypocrites, the unjust, the unwise virgins, and the goats.

And what are these doing, these evil workers, whose glory is in their shame, not only taking part in, but actually taking over, the Christian ministry? 'Whose glory is in their shame'?

Finally, as opposed to the apostle, his son Timothy, and all those ministers sent of Christ to follow Paul's example from the beginning, whose conversation was and is in heaven, from whence they looked and look for the Saviour, the Lord Jesus Christ, these 'evil workers', in total contrast, 'mind earthly things', Phil. 3:19.

But the apostle looked not on the things which can be seen, but on the things which cannot be seen, II Cor. 4:18. Those who followed the apostle, through his doctrine, were transformed by the renewing of their minds, Rom. 12:2, but the minds of those who followed the false teachers, who 'minded earthly things', never were transformed. They were worldly, conformed to this world, minding fleshly things, earthly things.

These earthly-minded false teachers sought the praise of man, their own advantage, and the whitewash of the hypocrite. They were carnally minded, were of the world, and the world heard them, and, after all, what else would one expect of evil workers, enemies of the cross of Christ, whose end is destruction, whose God is their belly, those whose mentality never rises above the flesh and this present world, who, in total contrast to the apostle and the apostolic ministry, 'minded earthly things', Phil. 3:19?

But one more example will suffice to show the nature and the deceit of those the avoidance of whom Paul declares to be a criterion of our safety. These 'evil workers', or, as Jesus names them, 'workers of iniquity', are described in the famous Sermon on the Mount, as it is said, 'Many will say to me in that day, Lord, Lord, have we not prophesied in thy name? and in thy name have cast out devils? and in thy name done many wonderful works?' Mt. 7:22.

Here you see that they lack not claim to miracles, who iniquitously rebel against the apostle, his doctrine, and the example of the apostolic ministry. They cover up their rebellion by claiming the signs of an apostle, whilst at the same time they revolt against the true apostolic authority.

But what miracle do we read of in Timothy? What miracle was ever wrought by Titus, Epaphras, Sylvanus, or any other whom the apostle counted as his sons in the ministry of the gospel? They were not apostles, but they were obedient to the apostles. Therefore they had no apostolic signs: what they had was apostolic obedience.

Hence, these evil workers pretend to signs and miracles, to disguise the fact that Christ had neither called them nor sent them, God had neither wrought in them nor spoken by them, and the Holy Ghost had neither verified their false doctrine nor anointed their corrupt preaching. Oh, but they would claim visions of the virgin; images of the saints; miracles in the grotto; and I know not what other fables, to beguile the simple.

And today, they will claim to prophesy in his name, speak tongues in gibberish, receive a spirit other than the Holy Spirit, heal the sick, change water into wine, or even raise the dead. And, if there be any other devilish blasphemy whereby they may say that God has done through them, for shame, no less than he did by Christ and his apostles, they will claim that also, finally to strut onto the stage at the last judgment with this brash familiarity: 'Lord, Lord!'

Then the truth will out: for they and their followers will hear the first, the last, and the only words Christ ever spoke to them in their whole lives, so to ring in their ears for the rest of eternity: 'I never knew you: depart from me, *ye that work iniquity*', Mt. 7:23.

And by this—that is, the claim to have performed apostolic miracles—no matter that deceitful and deceiving apostates of great evangelical repute have put their stamp on it, you may see that pentecostalism and the charismatic delusion are nothing but the deceit of evil workers. It is no different from the ancient Roman Catholic claimed sights and signs of the Madonna, or cures at Lourdes, or speaking in tongues at Avila, or preposterous fables concerning miracles from the relics of the saints.

Moreover you can see plainly that those who perpetrate and fabricate such absurd pretensions, whether ancient or modern, are nothing but what the apostle plainly calls 'evil workers', Phil. 3:2, on the one hand, and the Lord Jesus condemns as 'workers of iniquity', Mt. 7:23, on the other.

But there is a final group named by Paul to complete this unholy triad. They are called 'the concision', or, 'the mutilators'. The apostle employs a biting irony, a sarcasm that liberal evangelicals would not merely find distasteful, they would be moved to indignation—a rare performance—to say that it was positively unchristian, or 'unloving'. For by this cliché, as to the manner born, they reduce all character to a common absurdity.

But Almighty God and the Father; the Son of the living God, the Lord Jesus Christ; the Holy Ghost from heaven, the Spirit of truth, giving forth the sacred scripture of the new testament by the holy apostles, to whom its infallibility was entrusted, used the language 'Dogs; evil workers; the concision'. And who is he that will question that?

Why, the modern evangelical apostasy will question it. The love of God, of Christ, of the Spirit of truth, of the new testament, is not loving enough for them. But Paul with holy boldness sarcastically uses the parody 'concision' for 'circumcision' for two reasons.

First, circumcision never was an end in itself: it was a means to an end given to Abraham, of whom it is said 'He received the *sign* of circumcision', Rom. 4:11. But everybody knows the only value of a sign lies in the thing which it signifies.

And what did the sign of circumcision signify? That *the flesh had been taken away, cut off*, in the birth of Abraham's true seed. But the Jews were full of the flesh. Far from cutting off the flesh, they were nothing but flesh. Then their sign was worthless, nothing but a pointless mutilation.

Their sign was worthless: they were the concision: they mutilated themselves for nothing. 'If thou be a breaker of the law,
thy circumcision is made uncircumcision.' 'For he is not a
Jew, which is one outwardly; *neither is that circumcision, which
is outward in the flesh*: But he is a Jew, which is one inwardly;
and circumcision is that of the heart, in the spirit, and not in the
letter; whose praise is not of men, but of God', Rom. 2:28,29.

Now these legalistic hypocrites gloried in creeping into the
ecclesia, demanding the Gentile believers to be under the law
as a rule of life, and, to verify their subjection thereto, to
submit to circumcision. But Paul says, it is *not* circumcision: it
is concision, and they who do it are mutilators. Antinomian,
unevangelical, legalistic mutilators. And so are their Presby-
terian, Westminsterite, imitators who follow their false teaching
but deftly dispense with its sign.

Not only did these hypocrites, these whited sepulchres, fail
to keep the law themselves, but they turned it into an outward
show of forms and ceremonies, mutilating its true nature,
thus making themselves wholly offensive to God. They themselves never understood the circumcision which they demanded
of the Gentiles. For, if it signified not being born after the
flesh, it pointed to being born of God.

But these understood neither sign nor pointer, both of
which were fulfilled in the gospel of Christ. For Christ in the
cross *had* taken away the flesh, not in a sign but in the reality,
and, justified in him, *that true circumcision* was fulfilled already
in the Gentiles, who had been born of God: 'For we are the'
—true, inward—'circumcision, which worship God in the spirit,
and rejoice in Christ Jesus, and have no confidence in the
flesh', Phil. 3:3.

But this 'concision', these 'mutilators', insinuated themselves
into the church in Paul's absence, saying that 'The gospel was

all very well, but you must keep the law'—that is, their white-washed hypocritical outward form of it—'as a rule of life *as well*; and, as a sign of this, you must be circumcised.' Vile mutilators! Vile mutilators of law, of the gospel, of the sign, and of the thing signified. 'For Christ is the end of the law for righteousness to every one that believeth', Rom. 10:4, and 'In him also ye *are* circumcised with the circumcision made without hands', Col. 2:11.

What need then of mutilators? 'For we are the circumcision, which worship God in the spirit, and rejoice in Christ Jesus, and have no confidence in the flesh', Phil. 3:3. Then whether with the sign or without the sign; whether requiring circumcision or not requiring circumcision: Beware of dogs; beware of evil workers; beware of the concision, who would undo all that Christ has already accomplished for us in the cross, circumcision and all, besides totally delivering us from the law as such, whether under such euphemisms as 'a rule of life', or not: totally delivering us, 'that we might live unto God'.

Beware, I say, sign or not, beware as you would dread the very plague, beware of those who claim by the traditions of men—but contrary to the XIth of the Thirty-nine Articles—I say, beware of those who claim that the law, whilst not a rule of justification, is nevertheless a rule of life. If you receive that, you have been mutilated in your soul. Christ is our life, and Christ is all.

'I through the law am dead to the law, that I might live unto God. I am crucified with Christ', Gal. 2:19,20. And, if so, we are circumcised in him not by the sign, but in the reality, when he for us 'put off the body of the sin of the flesh by the circumcision of Christ', Col. 2:11, that is, through being made sin in his vicarious sacrifice at the cross.

But to this day there are those—not in the outward form of circumcision, now outmoded as a sign of being under the law to work for life—nevertheless, I say, there are those who, dispensing with the sign, would still bring us under bondage by the substance. The Substance? Yes, that we should walk by the law as a rule of life. And, compared to *that* enormity, what is the sign? Nothing. But the substance is a matter of life and death.

They say, It is a matter of life. Paul declares, The law brings nothing but wrath; it only genders a curse; it cannot give life; it shuts up to bondage; and is altogether and wholly a sentence of death.

All these defiant enemies who say otherwise are mutilators of our souls; butchers of the gospel; and Antinomian *charcutiers* against the law. They are called, The Concision. To this day. Saith the apostle, Beware of them.

For, says the apostle in his holy doctrine, 'Christ is the end of the law for righteousness to every one that believeth', Rom. 10:4; and, 'I through the law am dead to the law, that I might live unto God', Gal 2:19. 'Wherefore, my brethren, ye also are become dead to the law by the body of Christ; that ye should be married to another, even to him who is raised from the dead, that we should bring forth fruit unto God', Rom. 7:4.

So the apostle concludes, Rom. 7:6, 'But now we are delivered from the law, that being dead wherein we were held; that we should serve in newness of spirit, and not in the oldness of the letter.'

THE CONTENT OF PHILIPPIANS

Part Three
Philippians Ch. 3:3 to Ch. 4:23

'This one thing I do', Philippians 3:13

THIS passage, Ch. 3:3 to Ch. 4:23, takes us to the end of the epistle. The remarkable feature lies in the fact that the larger—and most outstanding—part of these verses forms a parenthesis. That is, the preponderance of this section effectively falls into brackets, it is an aside. This parenthesis takes in virtually the whole of Chapter 3 and a part of Chapter 4.

This is easily demonstrated by the observation that in Ch. 4:8 the apostle returns to the very same—and very final—words with which he had commenced in Ch. 3:1, 'Finally, my brethren'. As if—Ch. 3:1—he were about to conclude at that point. But this is not so. He *digresses* from that point, not to return to it until he repeats the words 'Finally, brethren' in Ch. 4:8.

But between the twofold use of the word 'Finally' lie twenty-eight verses. These twenty-eight verses span two chapters. It is evident that this section forms a parenthesis, a diversion, a parenthetical digression. But what started it? What is it about?

It is about safety. Safety started it. It is a digression on safety. 'For you it is safe', 3:1. Now, *nothing* is safe outside of Christ. Safety is only in Christ.

But how is one to be in Christ? If salvation is in none other, How may one win Christ? How may one be found in Christ? How may one know Christ? In a word, how may one be safe? Now, it is obvious that the answers to these questions more than warrant an aside, a parenthesis, interrupting the final conclusion of the epistle, and it is precisely that to which the Holy Ghost leads the apostle.

Paul's digression concerning safety points wholly to Christ, and it does so in terms of personal testimony. He tells the Philippians what he has done, is doing, and intends to do, concerning his safety, or salvation, in Christ, and at that in the most intimate and personal terms. Paul's resolution is threefold, and declares his single-minded determination and intention concerning Christ. First, as to winning Christ. Second, as to being found in Christ. And thirdly, as to knowing Christ.

The apostle shows that to speak of winning Christ is commensurate with losing everything that one might otherwise have gained for oneself in the flesh in this present world. Otherwise Christ cannot be won. Secondly, he declares that to speak of being found in Christ demands that one is not under the law, in any shape, or in any form, or at any time. Otherwise one cannot be found in Christ.

Finally the apostle demonstrates that to speak of knowing Christ involves the experimental consciousness of the power of his resurrection, that is, union with his life from the other side of death, and hence one is glad to embrace the fellowship of his sufferings, and to be made conformable unto his death. Otherwise one cannot know him.

From which it is evident that winning Christ cannot be achieved without being found in him; neither can there be any knowing of Christ except first it embrace both these previous and essential elements.

Moreover anything less than each and all of these inwoven essentials in the knowledge of Christ is to fall short—very far short—of safety, of salvation: in a word, to fail of the spiritual, evangelical, and experimental union that is in the Father and the Son.

In the first instance Paul introduces his determination to win Christ by declaring that this cannot be done in the flesh. 'For we are the circumcision, which worship God in the spirit, and rejoice in Christ Jesus, and *have no confidence in the flesh*', Phil. 3:3.

Twice more he refers to the flesh: 'Though I might have confidence in *the flesh*. If any man thinketh that he hath whereof he might trust in *the flesh*, I more', Phil. 3:4. He might once have had confidence, and so trusted, but now he utterly, absolutely, and continuously renounces the flesh, all trusting in the flesh, and any confidence in the flesh whatsoever. Why, Paul? 'That I may win Christ.' Otherwise, Christ cannot be won.

If perfection were to be obtained by or in the flesh, surely Paul appeared to be the most likely candidate. He lists his sevenfold fleshly qualifications: First, he was circumcised the eighth day; next, he was of the stock of Israel; third, he was of the tribe of Benjamin; again, he was an Hebrew of the Hebrews; then, as touching the law, he was a Pharisee; sixth, concerning zeal, he persecuted the church; and, seventh, touching the righteousness which is in the law, he was blameless.

Now here is fleshly perfection—sevenfold—in surfeit enough to outdo the carnal perfectionist notions both of John Wesley and the pope himself. Yes, but what is it all worth? Let us ask

Paul: What is it all worth Paul? How do you reckon up the value of this fleshly perfection so beloved of the Arminian, and so eulogized in the canonized saints of the papist calendar? 'I do count it but dung, that I may win Christ', Phil. 3:8.

'What things were gain to me, those I counted loss for Christ', Phil. 3:7. What things were gain to Paul? He was of the chosen seed; Paul could boast of the stock of Israel; of the tribe of Benjamin; of Jewish circumcision; of the straitest sect of the Jews' religion.

Paul gloried in the sanctity of the temple; in the ordained Levitical priesthood; the ceremonies and sacraments; the hallowed institutes of untold centuries. He possessed consuming zeal for what God had established by covenant. He kept himself blameless as to every point of rectitude in the law. He counted as gain his willing submission to the ancient traditions of the elders, besides the learned patriarchs of Jewish hierarchy.

These things were his birthright, it was in his blood, in his flesh, in the determination of his will, it was his by heritage in Abraham. Yes, Paul, but the children of God are born 'Not of blood, nor of the will of the flesh, nor of the will of man, but of God', John 1:13. 'Neither, because they are the seed of Abraham, are they all children: but, In Isaac shall thy seed be called. That is, They which are the children of the flesh, these are not the children of God', Rom. 9:7,8.

The children of the flesh not the children of God? And yet all your sevenfold perfection *was* in the flesh, Paul, as you testify yourself, 'If any man have whereof he might trust in the flesh, I more.' Yes, Paul, sevenfold more. But what was it all worth in the end? 'Dung', concludes Paul at the last.

But why? Because what Paul could never do in the flesh was beget *faith*. He could not believe. Why not? Because the flesh cannot believe. Another thing that Paul could never do in the flesh was to win Christ, because the flesh cannot win Christ. Yet another thing that Paul could never do in the flesh was see one single thing aright, because the flesh was blind, in darkness, and in a state of perpetual enmity.

First, the flesh cannot believe, neither can they that are in the flesh have any faith. 'Who *by him* do believe in God', says Peter, I Pet. 1:21, and if by him, then not of ourselves; and if not of ourselves, not of the flesh. All that the flesh can do is work, not believe, but Eph. 2:8,9, faith is the gift of God, not the work of the flesh; 'Not of works, lest any man should boast'.

Again, Jesus tells the Jews 'Therefore ye believe not, because ye are not of my sheep'. And if not of his sheep, then of the goats. Christ says the sheep believe. But the goats do not. They can neither work up faith nor so much as see what it is. Why not? Because it is exclusive to the sheep. Heb. 12:2 informs us that 'Christ is the author of our faith', and, in that case the flesh never wrote it. Christ wrote it, and wrote it on the heart of his own sheep. And none other.

II Pet. 1:1 assures those who are of the faith of God's elect that they 'have obtained' like precious faith with the apostles; not generated it: *obtained* it: therefore it was given to them. Whence it follows that faith is what the flesh can never produce, because, John 6:29, 'This is the work of God, that ye believe'; hence it is said, 'As many as were ordained to eternal life believed', Acts 13:48. And none other.

Next, The flesh cannot win Christ. 'So then it is not of him that willeth, nor of him that runneth, but of God that showeth mercy', Rom. 9:16. And, saith Jesus, 'Murmur not among yourselves. No man can come to me, except the Father which hath sent me draw him: and I will raise him up at the last day. It is written in the prophets, And they shall be all taught of God. Every man therefore that hath heard, and hath learned of the Father, cometh unto me', Jn. 6:43-45. And none other.

Again Jesus declares, 'Therefore said I unto you, that no man can come unto me, except it were given unto him of my Father', Jn. 6:65. And, if that be so, since, 'That which is born of the flesh is flesh, and that which is born of the Spirit is spirit', evidently none that are of the flesh can transform themselves into what they are not, for if they cannot receive the Spirit, being fleshly, then they can never win Christ, who is wholly spiritual.

Hence, in the flesh, Paul 'Verily thought that he ought'— mark that, ought, he felt obliged: it was his sense of duty— 'ought to do many things contrary to the name of Jesus', Acts 26:9. Such as 'Persecuting the church', Phil. 3:6; and keeping the clothes of those that stoned the first martyr, Stephen, lest these precious garments should be spattered with blood, Acts 7:58. And again, 'Making havoc of the church, entering into every house, and haling men and women committed them to prison', Acts 8:3.

All those things he did religiously, as his duty to God. From which we are to conclude that the flesh is not only incapable of faith, but, far from wishing to win Christ, although professing a false Christ, it is full of hatred to the true Christ, and every one of his disciples. Not only so: it remains blind and in the dark as to its real condition of implacable enmity towards the God it professes to worship.

'But their minds were blinded', saith Paul, II Cor. 3:14. And, 'If our gospel be hid, it is hid to them that are lost: in whom the god of this world hath blinded the minds of them which believe not', II Cor. 4:3,4. And will such as these seek to win Christ? No they will not. Then neither will any that are of the flesh. For that which is born of the flesh *is* flesh.

There is no beauty in Christ that they—who are of the flesh—should desire him, Isa. 53:2. How could any beauty be seen in the true Christ—whom they think of as false—when the flesh is blinded, darkened, and at its worst when most religious?

93

But, religious or not, 'To be fleshly minded is death', Rom. 8:6. 'Because the fleshly mind is enmity'—enmity itself—'against God: for it is not subject to the law of God, neither indeed can be. So then'—concludes the apostle—'they that are in the flesh cannot please God', Rom. 8:7,8. And if they cannot please God it is certain that, in the nature of the flesh, neither can they win Christ, nor have the least inclination to do so in truth.

No wonder that Paul renounced the flesh in its entirety, all confidence in the flesh absolutely, and any trust in the flesh continually, counted it all but dung. For so it is: a putrifying and stinking mass obnoxious even to human sight and smell, let alone the divine. Wherefore the carnal or fleshly nature will for ever keep from Christ, that is, save God intervene and draw of his own initiative and sheer mercy.

Then the clearest evidence of such grace will be the renunciation of the flesh, its confidence, and all its works, as we see in Paul, as an absolute necessity corresponding with the divinely inspired, spiritually inbreathed, heavenly generated aspiration to 'win Christ'.

In such a case, and in such a case alone, one observes the fulfilment of the true saying, 'He that loveth his life shall lose it; and he that hateth his life in this world shall keep it unto life eternal. If any man serve me, let him follow me; and where I am, there shall my servant be: if any man serve me, him will my Father honour', Jn. 12:25,26. Now, this is to win Christ of a truth.

But winning Christ is not all that is involved in the full knowledge of the Son of God. Equally intense was Paul's determination 'to be found in him', Phil. 3:9. However, this cannot be, without renouncing one's own righteousness: 'Not having mine own righteousness, which is of the law, but that which is through the faith of Christ, the righteousness which is of God by faith.'

Not that the self-righteousness of which Paul had before boasted through the law, was that of which the law approved. The Jews approved; the Pharisees approved; but neither the law, nor God approved. Why not? Because Paul's righteousness under the law was all outward form. It was blameless only in exterior conformity. But the law required inward purity. 'Woe unto you, scribes and Pharisees, hypocrites! for ye make clean the outside of the cup and of the platter, but within they are full of extortion and excess', Mt. 23:25.

Yet all the righteousness, the blamelessness, which Paul afore attained under the law, which now he calls dung, was that of outward appearance before men. But it was abomination in the sight of God. 'Woe unto you, scribes and Pharisees, hypocrites! for ye are like unto whited sepulchres, which indeed appear beautiful outward, but are within full of dead men's bones, and of all uncleanness. Even so ye also outwardly appear righteous unto men, but within ye are full of hypocrisy and iniquity', Mt. 23:27,28.

Nor can the legalist, or any who claim to walk by the law 'as a rule of life'—as they misname the sentence of death—ever attain to anything other than an outward show, which quite blinds their eyes to their own inward filth. But the law was given to reveal that inward filth, not for hypocrites to make a show of righteousness by misusing its pure commandments.

'For the law made nothing perfect', Heb. 7:19. 'Therefore by the deeds of the law there shall no flesh be justified in his sight: for by the law is the knowledge of sin', Rom. 3:20. The knowledge of sin, observe, not the knowledge of righteousness.

'For if righteousness come by the law, then Christ is dead in vain', Gal. 2:21. Then all Paul's previous vaunted righteousness and blamelessness, outward in the flesh, was in the sight of God abominable, and hypocritical, in that the spiritual purpose of the law was to teach man his helplessness under it:

'For we know that the law is spiritual; but I am carnal, sold under sin', Rom. 7:14.

Hence one must utterly renounce the law as a means by which one deludes oneself that by it righteousness might be attained, or life be given. One must come to own that under no circumstances can its rule be kept, confessing that it was never given to man as a rule of life at all, even as Paul declares, 'When we were in the flesh, the motions of sins, *which were by the law*, did work in our members *to bring forth fruit unto death*', Rom. 7:5. 'Because the law worketh wrath', Rom. 4:15, and nothing else.

The law is a killing letter; a sentence of death; a ministration of condemnation; and can bring nothing but the knowledge of sin and a dreadful curse. 'Cursed is every one that continueth not in all things which are written in the book of the law to do them. But that no man is justified by the law in the sight of God, it is evident: for, The just shall live by faith. And the law is not of faith: but, The man that doeth them shall live in them', Gal. 3:10-12. But Paul found that he could not live in them: he died by them, as he says, 'When the commandment came, sin revived, and I died', Rom. 7:9.

Wherefore he had renounced all legal righteousness, he had been delivered from the law, and hence no longer walked by it, being delivered from both its curse and its precept: For 'Christ hath redeemed us from the curse of the law, being made a curse for us: for it is written, Cursed is every one that hangeth on a tree', Gal. 3:13. And again, as to the precept, the law itself, 'God sent forth his Son, made of a woman, made under the law, to redeem them that were under the law, that we might receive the adoption of sons', Gal. 4:4,5; as he saith in another place, 'For ye are not under the law, but under grace', Rom. 6:14.

Thus Paul could say, 'I through the law am dead to the law, that I might live unto God', Gal. 2:19. And again, 'But now we are delivered from the law, that being dead wherein we were held', Rom. 7:6. Once more, Rom. 7:4, 'Wherefore, my brethren, ye also are become dead to the law by the body of Christ.' Now, if dead to the law, then dead to any attempt to attain or maintain righteousness by it, before or after justification. Dead is dead is dead.

And if this is not to renounce one's own righteousness for ever, What is? Even as Paul says 'Not having mine own righteousness which is of the law.' To be found in Christ of necessity therefore entails renunciation of legal righteousness, and, if so, full and final deliverance from the law itself must come first. But it did come first. Hence, Paul was found, and all who so follow him will be found, in Christ, even as it is said, 'And be found in him'.

What is it to be found in him? 'Not having mine own righteousness, which is of the law, but that which is through the faith of Christ, the righteousness which is of God by faith', Phil. 3:9. What righteousness is this, that is of God by faith?

It is imputed righteousness, 'Even as David also describeth the blessedness of the man, unto whom God imputeth righteousness without works, saying, Blessed are they whose iniquities are forgiven, and whose sins are covered. Blessed is the man to whom the Lord will not impute sin', Rom. 4:6-8. This is called the righteousness of faith. God wrought it, and God imputes it, and he does so to the ungodly and to sinners.

Of this, Abraham was an example: 'Abraham believed God, and it was counted unto him for righteousness. Now to him that worketh'—for righteousness, by the law—'is the reward' —of life—'not reckoned of grace, but of debt. But to him that worketh *not*, but *believeth on him that justifieth the ungodly*, his faith is counted for righteousness', Rom. 4:3-5.

This divine righteousness, which God freely reckons from heaven to the account of the ungodly on earth, is what Paul calls 'imputed righteousness'. This is that unique, divine righteousness which was wrought when Christ died, as it is said, 'Even the righteousness of God by faith of Jesus Christ', Rom. 3:22. This was obtained when Christ's blood was shed. And it is imputed when God brings the ungodly to faith.

This is that same righteousness of which Paul speaks when he says, Phil. 3:9, 'The righteousness which is through the faith of Christ, the righteousness which is of God by faith.' He to whom God has imputed this righteousness, who has been delivered from the law, who has thoroughly renounced his own righteousness, is the man of whom Paul speaks.

It is the position to which he himself aspires—and speaks for us all—when he declares his intention and determination 'to be found in him'. Being found in Christ therefore is a question of having the righteousness of God by faith of Jesus Christ imputed to one's account through faith in Christ's blood.

Faithfully to receive these things is to let the word of Christ dwell in us richly in all wisdom, so that we are enabled to sing with the spirit and with the understanding also:

'As touching righteousness of law,
  though blameless found thereby,
the things that once were gain to me
  for Christ count loss did I.

Yea, doubtless, and I count all things
  as nothing to afford,
to gain the knowledge excellent
  of Christ Jesus my Lord:

For whom moreover of all things
  I suffered have the loss:
and, that I may win Christ, them all
  do count but dung and dross;

And that I might be found in him,
  not having as mine own
the righteousness which to the law
  doth appertain alone;

But that which through the faith of Christ
  hath been by grace secured,
that is, the righteousness of faith
  which is approved of God:

That I may know him, and the power
  by which raised up was he,
that I his suff'rings' fellowship
  might know assuredly;

Not being made conformable
  unto his death in vain,
if I the resurrection might
  by any means attain.'

By these words from The Hymns of the New Testament we are led naturally into the third strand of that threefold cord which is not quickly broken, declared by Paul in his own testimony as his pursuit in life: that he might win Christ; that he might be found in him; and that he might know him. Each of these threefold strands having as its respective corollary the rejection of the flesh; the renunciation of legal righteousness; and the exercise of mortification unto life.

'That I may know him', Phil. 3:10, that is, not only about winning him, nor solely about righteousness in him, absolutely essential as are both of these things: they are composite strands. But not without this third criterion of the knowledge of Christ: here is the third strand that binds all; 'To know Christ.' To know him not for what he has done; not for the things concerning himself: but to know him in Person, by union and communion, as he is in and of himself.

That is, so to know him as one knows another face to face, heart to heart, and life to life; to know him personally. This completes the threefold cord. Less than this has a breaking strain unequal to the stress of the totality of the temptations, perplexities, cross providences, adverse persecutions and trials of this pilgrimage.

All of this, all three strands woven together, if it be maintained, if it be kept sound, if it reach to the end, has together a breaking strain nothing can overcome in heaven or on earth, this world or the next, no, not for time nor for eternity.

Thus to know him, is to be where he dwells: 'If I go and prepare a place for you'—in his Father's house—'I will come again' —in the Spirit, within—'and *receive you unto myself*; that where *I am*, there ye may be also', Jn. 14:3. Now to be where he is, with himself, of necessity must result in knowing him. Less near, further than this, is simply too distant, too impersonal. Too far away to result in the kind of knowledge of which Paul speaks.

'Yet a little while, and the world seeth me no more'—no: the world might have seen the apostles; the disciples; the one assembly: but that is the most that could have been seen—and, today, who could possibly see so much as that?—'yet the world seeth *me* no more; but *ye* see *me*'. Why? Because where he is, there they are also.

'Because I live, ye shall live also', saith Christ. This life is in the power of his resurrection, Phil. 3:10. 'At that day ye shall know that I am in my Father, and *ye in me*, and *I in you*', Jn. 14:19,20. Now, *this* is to know him, and it is the only way to know him: inwardly, by indwelling, by union, and in communion. 'That I may *know* him.'

'If a man love me, he will keep my words: and my Father will love him, and we will come unto him, and *make our abode with him*', Jn. 14:23. How could such a person, in such a case, fail to know him? '*Abide in me*, and *I in you*', Jn. 15:4. 'If a man abide not in me, he is cast forth as a branch'—no matter what else he has attained—'and is withered', Jn. 15:6. Here, it is either to abide in him, and know him; or it is not to abide in him, and never to know him.

To know him is inward: it is by the indwelling Spirit, whom he sends to dwell within: 'He shall glorify me: for he shall *receive of mine*'—in the glory—'and *show it unto you*'—on earth. 'A little while, and ye shall not see me: and again, a little while, and *ye shall see me*, because I go to the Father', Jn. 16:16.

When he ascended to the Father, in virtue of his atoning work on earth for his disciples, he received and sent forth the Spirit of truth, who dwelt within them. Then, one with that Spirit, spiritually Christ came to them, and dwelt in them, and they in him. This is to know him. Less, is not.

'That they all may be one: *as thou, Father, art in me*, and I in thee, *that they also may be one in us*'. Demonstrably this is not some future heavenly inheritance: it is *now*: 'that *the world* may believe that thou hast sent me'. Then this is to be fulfilled as a testimony to the world at present.

'And the glory which thou gavest me I have given them; that they may be one, even as we are one: *I in them, and thou in me*, that they may be made perfect in one.' *Now*. Now, so that 'The world may know that thou hast sent me.' Evidently this is intended to occur in the world at present, in order that the world may observe its visible effects. 'That the *world* may know that thou hast sent me, and hast loved them as thou hast loved me', Jn. 17:21-23.

'That the love wherewith thou hast loved me may be *in* them, and *I in them*', Jn. 17:26. Now, *this* is to know him, and it is the *only* way to know him, and it is what Paul meant when he said, '*That I may know him*', Phil. 3:10.

But just as Paul's speaking of winning Christ entailed the negative corollary of the loss of all things in the flesh; and just as Paul's speaking of being found in Christ correspondingly necessitated his not being found under the law; so here also, the knowing Christ—that is, in the power of his resurrection— of necessity required the parallel mortification of knowing also the fellowship of his sufferings, and the being made conformable unto his death.

As to knowing the power of Christ's resurrection, this is experimental. 'Like as Christ was raised up from the dead by the glory of the Father, we also should walk'—mark that, walk —'in newness of life', Rom. 6:4. For since we have been called to faith, and the Spirit has been given to us, and the life of Christ fills us, it follows that *life from the other side of death, more powerful than death*, dwells within us, who are his own. This is called, the *power* of his resurrection.

'If ye then be risen with Christ, seek those things which are above, where Christ sitteth on the right hand of God', Col. 3:1. And again, 'For ye are dead, and your life is *hid with Christ* in God', Col. 3:3. Hidden *within*. What is hidden within? Christ's risen life, flowing down from the heavenly glory by the Spirit, so to dwell within the saints. It is the *power* of this, not just the word of it, the *power* of it, that Paul desired to know: 'That I may know him, and the power of his resurrection', Phil. 3:10.

But I repeat: just as winning Christ entailed losing; just as being found in Christ involved renunciation; so knowing him necessitates mortification. This mortification comes by the actual experience of the fellowship of his sufferings. And this is the fellowship that comes from walking even as he walked. 'As he is, so are we in this world', I Jn. 4:17. This is what brings suffering.

First, What is meant by 'the fellowship of his sufferings'? Peter tells you: 'Forasmuch then as Christ hath *suffered* for us in the flesh, arm *yourselves* with the same mind', I Pet. 4:1. And again, I Pet. 2:21, 'Christ *suffered* for us, *leaving us an example*, that ye should follow his steps.' Not avoid them. Paul embraced those steps. But at the cost of suffering.

Every step of the pathway of Jesus on earth was one of suffering. He yearned to return to the glory of the Father in heaven: this world was alien to him: 'I am not of this world'. Hence he said, 'O faithless and perverse generation, how long shall I be with you? how long shall I suffer you?' Mt. 17:17. What loneliness was his: after all those years of ministry, how is it that he must needs say, and say to his disciples, 'Have I been so long time with you, and yet hast thou not known me?'

Jesus sighed. Jesus groaned within himself. Jesus wept. We do not read of his laughter. We read of his sweating as it were great drops of blood. He was a Man of Sorrows: 'Behold and see, if there be any sorrow like unto my sorrow.' Why? Because he did not belong here; because he dwelt and felt things in a dimension beyond the comprehension of the worldly. But not beyond the comprehension of the spiritual. Hence, 'That I may know him, and the power of his resurrection, and *the fellowship of his sufferings.*'

Paul fulfils the fellowship of Christ's sufferings where he speaks of 'My sufferings for you, filling up that which is behind of the afflictions of Christ in my flesh for his body's sake, which is the church', Col. 1:24.

He declares this fellowship, that of suffering, when he says, 'From henceforth let no man trouble me: for I bear in my body the marks of the Lord Jesus', Gal. 6:17. He tells of the sufferings of Christ abounding in him, II Cor. 1:5; of writing to the Corinthians out of much affliction and anguish of heart, with many tears, II Cor. 2:4.

He speaks of being 'troubled on every side, yet not distressed; perplexed, but not in despair; persecuted, but not forsaken;

cast down, but not destroyed.' Again, he tells of 'labours more abundant, stripes above measure, in prisons more frequent, in deaths oft. Of the Jews'—says he—'five times received I forty stripes save one.

'Thrice was I beaten with rods, once was I stoned, thrice I suffered shipwreck, a night and a day I have been in the deep; in journeyings often, in perils of waters, in perils of robbers, in perils by mine own countrymen, in perils by the heathen, in perils in the city, in perils in the wilderness, in perils in the sea, in perils among false brethren; in weariness and painfulness, in watchings often, in hunger and thirst, in fastings often, in cold and nakedness', II Cor. 11:23-27.

And not only Paul, for, 'All that will live godly in Christ Jesus shall *suffer* persecution', II Tim. 3:12. And, without exception, of all saints it is written, 'These are they which came out of great tribulation', Rev. 7:14. 'For unto you it is given in the behalf of Christ, not only to believe on him, but to *suffer* for his sake', Phil. 1:29.

Now, this is 'the fellowship of his sufferings', and Paul earnestly desired that not only he, but all saints, might be partakers thereof, as it is written, 'If we *suffer*, we shall also reign with him', II Tim. 2:12. But not if we do not, for if we do not suffer, it is certain, we shall never reign. Hence the apostle desired to know 'the fellowship of his sufferings'.

'Being made conformable unto his death', Phil. 3:10. This is passive. It is the result of that which God brings upon his people, they are *made* conformable unto Christ's death, meekly submitting to killing circumstances, mortifying humiliations, deadly persecutions, and crucifying providences. Yet they never break prison, never deliver themselves, but submit humbly to all the dispensations that befall them, by these things being *made* conformable unto his death.

'For whom the Lord loveth he chasteneth, and scourgeth every son whom he receiveth. If ye endure chastening, God dealeth with you as sons; for what son is he whom the father chasteneth not? But if ye be without chastisment, whereof all are partakers, then are ye bastards, and not sons', Heb. 12:6-8.

Hence Paul earnestly desired to be made conformable unto his death, 'Always bearing about in the body the dying of the Lord Jesus, that the life also of Jesus might be made manifest in our body', II Cor. 4:10. 'For if ye through the Spirit do mortify the deeds of the body, ye shall live', Rom. 8:13. 'Mortify therefore your members which are upon the earth', Col. 3:5.

See also how David submitted to the cruellest outward providences, causing him to die daily, yet he would never deliver himself, he always waited on the Lord, ever accepting everything as from his hand. As, for example, Psalm 11, Psalm 31, Psalm 35, Psalm 69, illustrate so poignantly.

Indeed saith Paul, 'I die daily'; more, 'I am crucified with Christ'; and again, 'God forbid that I should glory, save in the cross of our Lord Jesus Christ, by whom the world is crucified unto me, and I unto the world', Gal. 6:14. As he says in another place, 'They that are Christ's have crucified the flesh with the affections and lusts', Gal. 5:24. This is to die daily: it is meekly to be conformed to Christ's death, under the inward and outward dealings of God and the Father.

All this! All three strands of the threefold cord; and all at such price: each one so costly. Why Paul? 'If by any means I might attain unto the resurrection of the dead', Phil. 3:11. No presumption here. But, says one, Paul was an apostle! Yes? And so was Judas. Therefore Paul kept his body under, and brought it into subjection: lest by any means, after he had preached to others, he himself might be a castaway, I Cor. 9:27.

This was not to doubt God's election; Christ's redemption; or the Spirit's sealing: it was to show the essential fruits of all and to make manifest the necessary consequences of each. It was to distrust self, to judge one's own heart, to be aware of the deceitful corruption of the flesh, and to know experimentally the total depravity of human nature at its worst, that is, under the greatest gospel light.

There will be a resurrection of the just, as of the unjust. Just and unjust are *character* descriptions. They apply equally as much—more—to the just and unjust in religion. Just or unjust, righteous or unrighteous: the *character* determines the resurrection. Not profession or claimed position. The resurrection is of the evil, or of the good. It is of prior *character*. The *nature* of the life lived before death settles the resurrection from the dead. 'The evil and the good' is the criterion, not the profession of religion. Indeed, 'Judgment must *begin* at the house of God.'

'God will render to every man according to his *deeds*: to them who by patient continuance in well doing seek for glory and honour and immortality'—the resurrection of which Paul speaks, clearly manifesting his earnest desire to attain to it by answering to its foretold character—'eternal life: But unto them that are contentious, and do not obey the truth'—obey *this* truth, instead of contending against it—'indignation and wrath, tribulation and anguish', Rom. 2:6-9. 'For there is no respect of persons with God', Rom. 2:11.

Religion, Judaism, Christianity, evangelicalism, the Church, provide no cloak of theories or form of words, as if God could be mocked by outward appearances. He will not alter the sentence of justice for any profession of Christ, or any 'Lord, Lord', in the day of judgment. Not he that heareth these sayings of mine—saith Christ, in the Sermon on the Mount—but he that heareth *and doeth* them is approved.

There are foolish builders as well as wise; there are goats as well as sheep; there are foolish virgins as well as wise virgins. And by these things, by the *character* of them, the judgment will make manifest who are Christ's, and who are not.

Who? Why those that won him; those that are found in him; those that know him; those that embraced the fellowship of his sufferings, and were made conformable unto his death. These will shine out in the resurrection in consequence of their inwrought sanctification on earth. Character will make it manifest, and nothing other than character. That is what so-called 'evangelicalism' has missed entirely.

However, to live with this in one's eye, to have this as one's end, to attain this by any means—by winning, by losing; by being in him, by denying one's self; by knowing him, by living and dying with him: by *these* means, any and all of these means, by persevering and increasing in them, by every one of these means, the resurrection of the dead is attained.

Not by words. Not by the dead letter. But by being buried, by being raised, by enduring, by experiencing, by receiving not the word only, but the power also: so that the resurrection really makes manifest the life lived before it.

For this Paul panted: for it, he was on the stretch. He lived, breathed, existed *to be just* for that resurrection *of the just*. And by it he shamed the religious world, and every presumptuous false 'brother', let alone 'minister' or 'pastor', and brought down upon his head their undying hatred. But then, that is the fellowship of Christ's sufferings. 'If by any means I might attain unto the resurrection of the dead', Phil. 3:11.

O, I beseech you, do attend to the earnest panting of Paul after the resurrection. How he followed after, how with a single heart he could, and did, cry 'This one thing I do, forgetting those things which are behind, I press toward the mark of the high calling of God in Christ Jesus', Phil. 3:13,14.

How he called the brethren to be likeminded with him. How he besought them to be his followers; to use him as an example to follow; and as an example by which to judge deceivers, to follow whom was to end in certain perdition.

'For many walk, of whom I have told you often, and now tell you even weeping, that they are the enemies of the cross of Christ: whose end is destruction, whose God is their belly, and whose glory is in their shame, who mind earthly things', Phil. 3:18,19. Many so walked *then*. What of *now*?

If then Paul had no man likeminded, if then he urged them to take him for an example in life, doctrine, ordinance, fellowship, and experience, if then he entreated the saints not to be deceived, because many deceivers swarmed into the churches *then*, what of *now*? We cannot expect it to be *better* at the end: only *infinitely worse*.

But we have our example. And for my part, would God I might follow it more perfectly, emulate it more exactly, embody it more totally. So that—instead of in any way hindering—my weeping, yearning, praying, watching, fasting, love might stimulate others to turn *wholly* from *all* deceivers, so as to say, 'Brethren, be followers together of me, and mark them which walk so as ye have us for an ensample', Phil. 3:17.

For we are not enemies of the cross of Christ: we preach Christ crucified, and at that, according to the true doctrine of the gospel. Our God is not our belly, but our God is the God of glory, who raised Christ from the dead according to our gospel. Our glory is not in our shame, but our God is our glory. God forbid that we should glory, save in the cross of our Lord Jesus Christ, by which the world is crucified unto us and we unto the world.

We do not mind earthly things: we mind spiritual things; for to be carnally minded is death, but to be spiritually minded is life and peace. Indeed, we are transformed by the renewing of our mind, having the mind of Christ, God is witness. For our conversation is in heaven: thence our life, our existence, our being, our concentration, our direction.

We are always looking up to heaven, any day, any hour, any minute, any moment, we look for and expect the Saviour, our Lord Jesus Christ, at his tremendous heaven-rending, earth-dissolving, element-melting appearance to judge the quick and the dead. We look for him in whom we trust, live, move, and hope to attain the resurrection of the dead.

That is, we look for the resurrection of the just, of the sons of God, in which the elect put off this vile body—Oh, how vile it is, what a foul enemy, without and within, how hardly do we mortify it, how clamorous is its deadly false life, how we long to put it off—who shall change this vile body, that it may be fashioned like unto his glorious body.

This is the resurrection. Of the body. But no longer vile. Then radiant, in light presently unbearable, in glory now unimaginable, fashioned like unto his glorious body, according to the working whereby he is able even to subdue all things unto himself, to whom be glory and dominion for ever. Amen.

The first seven verses of Philippians Chapter 4 provide an exhortation resulting from the testimony of Chapter 3. Thence follows an entreaty for unity between two women; next an appeal to Epaphroditus to help those women who laboured with Paul in the gospel, with Clement also, and others Paul's fellowlabourers, whose names are in the book of life.

In verse 4 Paul reiterates his constant theme: 'Rejoice in the Lord alway: and again I say, Rejoice.' His mind, his conversation, in heaven, he feels the Lord at hand:

> 'Your moderation in all things
>   to all make known do ye;
> the Lord himself is near at hand:
>   for nothing careful be.
>
> But let in everything by prayer
>   and supplication made
> with all thanksgiving, your requests
>   be unto God conveyed.

> And so God's peace, which doth surpass
> all understanding deep,
> shall through Christ Jesus all your hearts
> and minds securely keep.'

In verse 8 the apostle closes the parenthesis, or digression, commenced after the words of Ch. 3:1, 'Finally, my brethren'. He returns to this conclusion, Ch. 4:8, 'Finally, brethren'.

Chapter 4 finishes briefly. There is to be exercise of mind to virtue and praise. Brethren are to follow Paul in all things, the God of peace attendant. In verses 10 to 20, the apostle gives thanks—in a way at once most spiritual and edifying—for the gift sent by the hand of Epaphroditus from the Philippians to Paul.

And, indeed, how grateful we should be for their liberality also, since the same gift was the moving cause of this epistle having been written. In the last three verses Paul conveys his concluding salutations and benediction.

However, it is seemly that we should return to Philippians 4:8, in the words of The Hymns of the New Testament. With this conclusion there lingers the sweet fragrance of Christ in the heart, mind and memory:

> 'Now, brethren, whatsoever things
>   there are of verity,
> what things soever honest are,
>   or what things just that be;
>
> Whatever things are pure, or what
>   in loveliness are wrought,
> or whatsoever things ye hear
>   that be of good report;
>
> If there be any virtue found,
>   if there be any praise,
> then meditate upon these things,
>   and think on them always.'

JOHN METCALFE

INDEX

TO OTHER PUBLICATIONS

PSALMS, HYMNS AND SPIRITUAL SONGS

THE PSALMS
OF THE
OLD TESTAMENT

The Psalms of the Old Testament, the result of years of painstaking labour, is an original translation into verse from the Authorised Version, which seeks to present the Psalms in the purest scriptural form possible for singing. Here, for the first time, divine names are rendered as and when they occur in the scripture, the distinction between LORD and Lord has been preserved, and every essential point of doctrine and experience appears with unique perception and fidelity.

The Psalms of the Old Testament is the first part of a trilogy written by John Metcalfe, the second part of which is entitled *Spiritual Songs from the Gospels*, and the last, *The Hymns of the New Testament*. These titles provide unique and accurate metrical versions of passages from the psalms, the gospels and the new testament epistles respectively, and are intended to be used together in the worship of God.

Price £2.50 *(postage extra)*
(hard-case binding, dust-jacket)
Printed, sewn and bound
by the John Metcalfe Publishing Trust
ISBN 0 9506366 7 3

SPIRITUAL SONGS

FROM

THE GOSPELS

The *Spiritual Songs from the Gospels*, the result of years of painstaking labour, is an original translation into verse from the Authorised Version, which seeks to present essential parts of the gospels in the purest scriptural form possible for singing. The careful selection from Matthew, Mark, Luke and John, set forth in metrical verse of the highest integrity, enables the singer to sing 'the word of Christ' as if from the scripture itself, 'richly and in all wisdom'; and, above all, in a way that facilitates worship in song of unprecedented fidelity.

The *Spiritual Songs from the Gospels* is the central part of a trilogy written by John Metcalfe, the first part of which is entitled *The Psalms of the Old Testament*, and the last, *The Hymns of the New Testament*. These titles provide unique and accurate metrical versions of passages from the psalms, the gospels and the new testament epistles respectively, and are intended to be used together in the worship of God.

Price £2.50 *(postage extra)*
(hard-case binding, dust-jacket)
Printed, sewn and bound
by the John Metcalfe Publishing Trust
ISBN 0 9506366 8 1

THE HYMNS

OF THE

NEW TESTAMENT

The *Hymns of the New Testament*, the result of years of painstaking labour, is an original translation into verse from the Authorised Version, which presents essential parts of the new testament epistles in the purest scriptural form possible for singing. The careful selection from the book of Acts to that of Revelation, set forth in metrical verse of the highest integrity, enables the singer to sing 'the word of Christ' as if from the scripture itself, 'richly and in all wisdom'; and, above all, in a way that facilitates worship in song of unprecedented fidelity.

The *Hymns of the New Testament* is the last part of a trilogy written by John Metcalfe, the first part of which is entitled *The Psalms of the Old Testament*, and the next, *Spiritual Songs from the Gospels*. These titles provide unique and accurate metrical versions of passages from the psalms, the gospels and the new testament epistles respectively, and are intended to be used together in the worship of God.

Price £2.50 *(postage extra)*
(hard-case binding, dust-jacket)
Printed, sewn and bound
by the John Metcalfe Publishing Trust
ISBN 0 9506366 9 X

'THE APOSTOLIC FOUNDATION
OF THE
CHRISTIAN CHURCH' SERIES

Third Printing

FOUNDATIONS UNCOVERED

THE APOSTOLIC FOUNDATION
OF THE
CHRISTIAN CHURCH

Volume I

Foundations Uncovered is the introduction to the major series: 'The Apostolic Foundation of the Christian Church'.

Rich in truth, the Introduction deals comprehensively with the foundation of the apostolic faith under the descriptive titles: The Word, The Doctrine, The Truth, The Gospel, The Faith, The New Testament, and The Foundation.

The contents of the book reveal: The Fact of the Foundation; The Foundation Uncovered; What the Foundation is not; How the Foundation is Described; and, Being Built upon the Foundation.

'This book comes with the freshness of a new Reformation.'

Price 75p *(postage extra)*
(Laminated cover)
Printed, sewn and bound
by the John Metcalfe Publishing Trust
ISBN 0 9506366 5 7

*Thoroughly revised and extensively rewritten
second edition*

Third Printing

THE BIRTH OF JESUS CHRIST

THE APOSTOLIC FOUNDATION
OF THE
CHRISTIAN CHURCH

Volume II

'The very spirit of adoration and worship rings through the pages of *The Birth of Jesus Christ.*

'The author expresses with great clarity the truths revealed to him in his study of holy scriptures at depth. We are presented here with a totally lofty view of the Incarnation.

'John Metcalfe is to be classed amongst the foremost expositors of our age; and his writings have about them that quality of timelessness that makes me sure they will one day take their place among the heritage of truly great Christian works.'

From a review by Rev. David Catterson.

'Uncompromisingly faithful to scripture ... has much to offer which is worth serious consideration ... deeply moving.'

The Expository Times.

Price 95p *(postage extra)*
(Laminated Cover)
Printed, sewn and bound
by the John Metcalfe Publishing Trust
ISBN 1 870039 48 3

*Thoroughly revised and extensively rewritten
second edition*

Third Printing

THE MESSIAH

THE APOSTOLIC FOUNDATION
OF THE
CHRISTIAN CHURCH

Volume III

The Messiah is a spiritually penetrating and entirely original
exposition of Matthew chapter one to chapter seven from the
trenchant pen of John Metcalfe.

Matthew Chapters One to Seven

GENEALOGY · BIRTH · STAR OF BETHLEHEM
HEROD · FLIGHT TO EGYPT · NAZARETH
JOHN THE BAPTIST · THE BAPTIST'S MINISTRY
JESUS' BAPTISM · ALL RIGHTEOUSNESS FULFILLED
HEAVEN OPENED · THE SPIRIT'S DESCENT
THE TEMPTATION OF JESUS IN THE WILDERNESS
JESUS' MANIFESTATION · THE CALLING · THE TRUE DISCIPLES
THE BEATITUDES · THE SERMON ON THE MOUNT

'Something of the fire of the ancient Hebrew prophet ....
Metcalfe has spiritual and expository potentials of a high order.'

The Life of Faith.

Price £7.75 *(postage extra)*
Hardback 420 pages
Laminated bookjacket
Printed, sewn and bound
by the John Metcalfe Publishing Trust
ISBN 1 870039 51 3

THE SON OF GOD AND SEED OF DAVID

THE APOSTOLIC FOUNDATION
OF THE
CHRISTIAN CHURCH

Volume IV

The Son of God and Seed of David is the fourth volume in the major work entitled 'The Apostolic Foundation of the Christian Church.'

'The author proceeds to open and allege that Jesus Christ is and ever was *The Son of God*. This greatest of subjects, this most profound of all mysteries, is handled with reverence and with outstanding perception.

'The second part considers *The Seed of David*. What is meant precisely by 'the seed'? And why 'of David'? With prophetic insight the author expounds these essential verities.'

Price £6.95 *(postage extra)*
Hardback 250 pages
Laminated bookjacket
Printed, sewn and bound
by the John Metcalfe Publishing Trust
ISBN 1 870039 16 5

CHRIST CRUCIFIED

THE APOSTOLIC FOUNDATION
OF THE
CHRISTIAN CHURCH

Volume V

Christ Crucified the definitive work on the crucifixion, the blood, and the cross of Jesus Christ.

The crucifixion of Jesus Christ witnessed in the Gospels: the gospel according to Matthew; Mark; Luke; John.

The blood of Jesus Christ declared in the Epistles: the shed blood; the blood of purchase; redemption through his blood; the blood of sprinkling; the blood of the covenant.

The doctrine of the cross revealed in the apostolic foundation of the Christian church: the doctrine of the cross; the cross and the body of sin; the cross and the carnal mind; the cross and the law; the offence of the cross; the cross of our Lord Jesus Christ.

Price £6.95 *(postage extra)*
Hardback 300 pages
Laminated bookjacket
Printed, sewn and bound
by the John Metcalfe Publishing Trust
ISBN 1 870039 08 4

JUSTIFICATION BY FAITH

THE APOSTOLIC FOUNDATION
OF THE
CHRISTIAN CHURCH

Volume VI

THE HEART OF THE GOSPEL · THE FOUNDATION OF THE CHURCH
THE ISSUE OF ETERNITY
CLEARLY, ORIGINALLY AND POWERFULLY OPENED

The basis · The righteousness of the law
The righteousness of God · The atonement · Justification
Traditional views considered · Righteousness imputed to faith
Faith counted for righteousness · Justification by Faith

'And it came to pass, when Jesus had ended these sayings, the people were astonished at his doctrine: for he taught them as one having authority, and not as the scribes.' Matthew 7:28,29.

Price £7.50 *(postage extra)*
Hardback 375 pages
Laminated bookjacket
Printed, sewn and bound
by the John Metcalfe Publishing Trust
ISBN 1870039 11 4

THE CHURCH: WHAT IS IT?

THE APOSTOLIC FOUNDATION
OF THE
CHRISTIAN CHURCH

Volume VII

The answer to this question proceeds first from the lips of Jesus himself, Mt. 16:18, later to be expounded by the words of the apostles whom he sent.

Neither fear of man nor favour from the world remotely affect the answer.

Here is the truth, the whole truth, and nothing but the truth.

The complete originality, the vast range, and the total fearlessness of this book command the attention in a way that is unique.

Read this book: you will never read another like it.

Outspokenly devastating yet devastatingly constructive.

Price £7.75 *(postage extra)*
Hardback 400 pages
Laminated bookjacket
Printed, sewn and bound
by the John Metcalfe Publishing Trust
ISBN 1 870039 23 8

OTHER TITLES

NOAH AND THE FLOOD

Noah and the Flood expounds with vital urgency the man and the message that heralded the end of the old world. The description of the flood itself is vividly realistic. The whole work has an unmistakable ring of authority, and speaks as 'Thus saith the Lord'.

'Mr. Metcalfe makes a skilful use of persuasive eloquence as he challenges the reality of one's profession of faith ... he gives a rousing call to a searching self-examination and evaluation of one's spiritual experience.'
The Monthly Record of the Free Church of Scotland.

Price £1.90 *(postage extra)*
(Laminated Cover)
Printed, sewn and bound
by the John Metcalfe Publishing Trust
ISBN 1 870039 22 X

DIVINE FOOTSTEPS

Divine Footsteps traces the pathway of the feet of the Son of man from the very beginning in the prophetic figures of the true in the old testament through the reality in the new; doing so in a way of experimental spirituality. At the last a glimpse of the coming glory is beheld as his feet are viewed as standing at the latter day upon the earth.

Price 95p *(postage extra)*
(Laminated Cover)
Printed, sewn and bound
by the John Metcalfe Publishing Trust
ISBN 1 870039 21 1

THE RED HEIFER

The Red Heifer was the name given to a sacrifice used by the children of Israel in the Old Testament—as recorded in Numbers 19—in which a heifer was slain and burned. Cedar wood, hyssop and scarlet were cast into the burning, and the ashes were mingled with running water and put in a vessel. It was kept for the children of Israel for a water of separation: it was a purification for sin.

In this unusual book the sacrifice is brought up to date and its relevance to the church today is shown.

Price 75p *(postage extra)*
ISBN 0 9502515 4 2

THE WELLS OF SALVATION

The Wells of Salvation is written from a series of seven powerful addresses preached at Tylers Green. It is a forthright and experimental exposition of Isaiah 12:3, 'Therefore with joy shall ye draw water out of the wells of salvation.'

John Metcalfe is acknowledged to be perhaps the most gifted expositor and powerful preacher of our day and this is to be seen clearly in The Wells of Salvation.

Price £1.50 *(postage extra)*
(Laminated Cover)
ISBN 0 9502515 6 9

OF GOD OR MAN?

LIGHT FROM GALATIANS

The Epistle to the Galatians contends for deliverance from the law and from carnal ministry.

The Apostle opens his matter in two ways:

Firstly, Paul vindicates himself and his ministry against those that came not from God above, but from Jerusalem below.

Secondly, he defends the Gospel and evangelical liberty against legal perversions and bondage to the flesh.

Price £1.45 *(postage extra)*
(Laminated Cover)
ISBN 0 9506366 3 0

A QUESTION FOR POPE JOHN PAUL II

As a consequence of his many years spent apart in prayer, lonely vigil, and painstaking study of the scripture, John Metcalfe asks a question and looks for an answer from Pope John Paul II.

Price £1.25. *(postage extra)*
(Laminated Cover)
ISBN 0 9506366 4 9

THE BOOK OF RUTH

The Book of Ruth is set against the farming background of old testament Israel at the time of the Judges, the narrative—unfolding the work of God in redemption—being marked by a series of agricultural events.

These events—the famine; the barley harvest; the wheat harvest; the winnowing—possessed a hidden spiritual significance to that community, but, much more, they speak in figure directly to our own times, as the book reveals.

Equally contemporary appear the characters of Ruth, Naomi, Boaz, and the first kinsman, drawn with spiritual perception greatly to the profit of the reader.

Price £4.95 *(postage extra)*
Hardback 200 pages
Laminated bookjacket
Printed, sewn and bound
by the John Metcalfe Publishing Trust
ISBN 1 870039 17 3

PRESENT-DAY CONVERSIONS
OF THE NEW TESTAMENT KIND

FROM THE MINISTRY OF
JOHN METCALFE

The outstandingly striking presentation of this fascinating paperback will surely catch the eye, as its title and contents will certainly captivate the mind: here is a unique publication.

Woven into a gripping narrative, over twenty-one short life stories, all centred on conversions that simply could not have happened had not God broken in, and had not Christ been revealed, the book presents a tremendous challenge, at once moving and thrilling to the reader.

Price £2.25 *(postage extra)*
(Laminated Cover)
Printed, sewn and bound
by the John Metcalfe Publishing Trust
ISBN 1 870039 31 9

DIVINE MEDITATIONS

OF

WILLIAM HUNTINGTON

Originally published by Mr. Huntington as a series of letters to J. Jenkins, under the title of 'Contemplations on the God of Israel', the spiritual content of this correspondence has been skilfully and sympathetically edited, abridged, and arranged so as to form a series of meditations, suitable for daily readings.

Mr. Huntington's own text is thereby adapted to speak directly to the reader in a way much more suited to his ministering immediately to ourselves, in our own circumstances and times.

It is greatly hoped that many today will benefit from this adaption which carefully retains both the spirit and the letter of the text. If any prefer the original format, this is readily available from several sources and many libraries.

Nevertheless, the publishers believe the much more readable form into which Mr. Huntington's very words have been adapted will appeal to a far wider audience, for whose comfort and consolation this carefully edited work has been published.

Price £2.35 (postage extra)
(Laminated Cover)
Printed, sewn and bound
by the John Metcalfe Publishing Trust
ISBN 1 870039 24 6

SAVING FAITH

The sevenfold work of the Holy Ghost in bringing a sinner to saving faith in Christ opened and enlarged.

True faith is the work of God. False faith is the presumption of man. But where is the difference? *Saving Faith* shows the difference.

Price £2.25 *(postage extra)*
Paperback 250 pages
(Laminated Cover)
Printed, sewn and bound
by the John Metcalfe Publishing Trust
ISBN 1 870039 40 8

DELIVERANCE FROM THE LAW
THE WESTMINSTER CONFESSION EXPLODED

Deliverance from the law. A devastating vindication of the gospel of Christ against the traditions of man.

Price £1.90 *(postage extra)*
Paperback 160 pages
(Laminated Cover)
Printed, sewn and bound
by the John Metcalfe Publishing Trust
ISBN 1 870039 41 6

NEWLY PUBLISHED

THE BEATITUDES

A unique insight destined to be the classic opening of this
wonderful sequence of utterances from the lips of Jesus.

The reader will discover a penetration of the spiritual heights
and divine depths of these peerless words in a way ever fresh
and always rewarding though read time and time again.

Price £1.90 *(postage extra)*
Paperback 185 pages
(Laminated cover)
Printed, sewn and bound
by the John Metcalfe Publishing Trust
ISBN 1 870039 45 9

NEWLY PUBLISHED

COLOSSIANS

This concise and unique revelation of the Epistle to the Colossians has the hallmark of spiritual originality and insight peculiar to the ministry of John Metcalfe. It is as if a diamond, inert and lifeless in itself, has been divinely cut at great cost, so that every way in which it is turned, the light from above is enhanced and magnified to break forth with divine radiance showing colour and depth hitherto unsuspected.

The Trustees give glory and thanks to God for the privilege of producing and subsidising this work.

Price 95p *(postage extra)*
Paperback 135 pages
(Laminated cover)
Printed, sewn and bound
by the John Metcalfe Publishing Trust
ISBN 1 870039 55 6

NEWLY PUBLISHED
PHILIPPIANS

The Epistle of Paul the Apostle to the Philippians is opened
by this work from the pen of John Metcalfe with that lucid
thoroughness which one has come to expect from a ministry
received 'not of men, neither by man, but by the revelation of
Jesus Christ'.

The work of God at Philippi is traced 'from the first day' until
the time at which the epistle was written. Never were Lydia
or the Philippian jailor drawn with more lively insight. The
epistle itself is revealed in order, with passages—such as 'the
mind that was in Christ Jesus'—that evidence the work of no
less than a divine for our own times.

The Trustees give glory and thanks to God for the privilege
of producing and subsidising this book.

Price £1.90 (postage extra)
Paperback 185 pages
(Laminated cover)
Printed, sewn and bound
by the John Metcalfe Publishing Trust
ISBN 1 870039 56 4

'TRACT FOR THE TIMES' SERIES

THE GOSPEL OF GOD

'TRACT FOR THE TIMES' SERIES

The Gospel of God. Beautifully designed, this tract positively describes the gospel under the following headings: The Gospel is of God; The Gospel is Entirely of God; The Gospel is Entire in Itself; The Gospel is Preached; The Gospel Imparts Christ; and, Nothing But the Gospel Imparts Christ.

Price 25p *(postage extra)*
(Laminated Cover)
No. 1 in the Series

THE STRAIT GATE

'TRACT FOR THE TIMES' SERIES

The Strait Gate. Exceptionally well made, this booklet consists of extracts from 'The Messiah', compiled in such a way as to challenge the shallowness of much of today's 'easy-believism', whilst positively pointing to the strait gate.

Price 25p *(postage extra)*
(Laminated Cover)
No. 2 in the Series

ETERNAL SONSHIP
AND TAYLOR BRETHREN

'TRACT FOR THE TIMES' SERIES

Eternal Sonship and Taylor Brethren. This booklet is highly recommended, particularly for those perplexed by James Taylor's teaching against the eternal sonship of Christ.

Price 25p *(postage extra)*
(Laminated Cover)
No. 3 in the Series

MARKS OF THE
NEW TESTAMENT CHURCH

'TRACT FOR THE TIMES' SERIES

Marks of the New Testament Church. This exposition from Acts 2:42 declares what were, and what were not, the abiding marks of the church. The apostles' doctrine, fellowship and ordinances are lucidly explained.

Price 25p *(postage extra)*
(Laminated Cover)
No. 4 in the Series

THE CHARISMATIC DELUSION

'TRACT FOR THE TIMES' SERIES

The Charismatic Delusion. A prophetic message revealing the fundamental error of this movement which has swept away so many in the tide of its popularity. Here the delusion is dispelled.

Price 25p *(postage extra)*
(Laminated Cover)
No. 5 in the Series

PREMILLENNIALISM EXPOSED

'TRACT FOR THE TIMES' SERIES

Premillennialism Exposed. Well received evangelically, particularly through the influence of J.N. Darby, the Schofield bible, and the Plymouth Brethren, Premillennialism has assumed the cloak of orthodoxy. In this tract the cloak is removed, and the unorthodoxy of this system is exposed. A remarkable revelation.

Price 25p *(postage extra)*
(Laminated Cover)
No. 6 in the Series

JUSTIFICATION AND PEACE

'TRACT FOR THE TIMES' SERIES

Justification and Peace. This tract is taken from a message preached in December 1984 at Penang Hill, Malaysia. In this well-known address, peace with God is seen to be based upon nothing save justification by faith. No one should miss this tract.

Price 25p *(postage extra)*
(Laminated Cover)
No. 7 in the Series

FAITH OR PRESUMPTION?

'TRACT FOR THE TIMES' SERIES

Faith or presumption? The eighth tract in this vital series exposes the difference between faith and presumption, showing that faith is not of the law, neither is is apart from the work of God, nor is it of man. The work of God in man that precedes saving faith is opened generally and particularly, and the tract goes on to reveal positively the nature of saving faith. Belief and 'easy-believism' are contrasted, making clear the difference between the two, as the system of presumption—called easy-believism—is clearly shown, and the way of true belief pointed out with lucid clarity.

Price 25p *(postage extra)*
(Laminated Cover)
No. 8 in the Series

THE ELECT UNDECEIVED
'TRACT FOR THE TIMES' SERIES

The Elect undeceived, the ninth Tract for the Times, earnestly contends for 'the faith once delivered to the saints' in a way that is spiritually edifying, positive, and subject to the Lord Jesus Christ according to the scriptures.

The Tract is a response to the pamphlet 'Salvation and the Church' published jointly by the Catholic Truth Society and Church House Publishing, in which the Anglican and Roman Catholic Commissioners agree together about JUSTIFICATION. The pamphlet shows how they have agreed.

Price 25p *(postage extra)*
(Laminated Cover)
No. 9 in the Series

JUSTIFYING RIGHTEOUSNESS
'TRACT FOR THE TIMES' SERIES

Justifying Righteousness. Was it wrought by the law of Moses or by the blood of Christ? Written not in the language of dead theology but that of the living God, here is the vital and experimental doctrine of the new testament. Part of the book 'Justification by Faith', nevertheless this tract has a message in itself essential to those who would know and understand the truth.

Price 25p *(postage extra)*
(Laminated Cover)
No. 10 in the Series

RIGHTEOUSNESS IMPUTED

'TRACT FOR THE TIMES' SERIES

Righteousness Imputed. The truth of the gospel and the fallacy of tradition. Here the gospel trumpet of the jubilee is sounded in no uncertain terms, as on the one hand that truth essential to be believed for salvation is opened from holy scripture, and on the other the errors of Brethrenism are brought to light in a unique and enlightening way. This tract is taken from the book 'Justification by Faith', but in itself it conveys a message of great penetration and clarity.

Price 25p *(postage extra)*
(Laminated Cover)
No. 11 in the Series

THE GREAT DECEPTION

'TRACT FOR THE TIMES' SERIES

The Great Deception. The erosion of Justification by faith. All ministers, every Christian, and each assembly ought not only to possess but to read and reread this prophetic message as the word of the Lord to this generation, set in the context of the age. This tract is part of the book 'Justification by Faith' but contains within itself a message which is at once vital and authoritative.

Price 25p *(postage extra)*
(Laminated Cover)
No. 12 in the Series

A FAMINE IN THE LAND

'TRACT FOR THE TIMES' SERIES

A Famine in the Land. Taken from the Book of Ruth, with telling forcefulness this tract opens conditions exactly parallel to those of our own times. 'Behold, the days come, saith the Lord GOD, that I will send a famine in the land, not a famine of bread, nor a thirst for water, but of hearing the words of the LORD: and they shall wander from sea to sea, and from the north even to the east, they shall run to and fro to seek the word of the LORD, and shall not find it.'

Price 25p *(postage extra)*
(Laminated Cover)
No. 13 in the Series

BLOOD AND WATER

'TRACT FOR THE TIMES' SERIES

Blood and Water. Of the four gospels, only John reveals the truth that blood was shed at the cross. When it was shed, Jesus was dead already. With the blood there came forth water. But what do these things mean? With devastating present-day application, this tract tells you what they mean.

Price 25p *(postage extra)*
(Laminated Cover)
No. 14 in the Series

WOMEN BISHOPS?

'TRACT FOR THE TIMES' SERIES

Women Bishops? This is a question that has arisen in America, but should it have arisen at all?
Read this tract and find out the authoritative answer.

Price 25p *(postage extra)*
(Laminated Cover)
No. 15 in the Series

THE HEAVENLY VISION

'TRACT FOR THE TIMES' SERIES

The Heavenly Vision not only transformed the prophet himself, it became a savour of life unto life—or death unto death—to all the people.
'*Where there is no vision the people perish*', Proverbs 29:18. This is true. But where is the vision today? And what is the vision today? This tract answers those questions.

Price 25p *(Postage extra)*
(Laminated Cover)
No. 16 in the Series

xl

EVANGELICAL TRACTS

EVANGELICAL TRACTS

1. **The Two Prayers of Elijah.** Green card cover, price 10p.

2. **Wounded for our Transgressions.** Gold card cover, price 10p.

3. **The Blood of Sprinkling.** Red card cover, price 10p.

4. **The Grace of God that brings Salvation.** Blue card cover, price 10p.

5. **The Name of Jesus.** Rose card cover, price 10p.

6. **The Ministry of the New Testament.** Purple card cover, price 10p.

7. **The Death of the Righteous** (*The closing days of J.B. Stoney*) by A.M.S. (his daughter). Ivory card cover, Price 10p.

8. **Repentance.** Sky blue card cover, price 10p.

9. **Legal Deceivers Exposed.** Crimson card cover, price 10p.

10. **Unconditional Salvation.** Green card cover, price 10p.

11. **Religious Merchandise.** Brown card cover, price 10p.

12. **Comfort.** Pink card cover, price 10p.

13. **Peace.** Grey card cover, price 10p.

14. **Eternal Life.** Cobalt card cover, price 10p.

ECCLESIA TRACTS

ECCLESIA TRACTS

The Beginning of the Ecclesia by John Metcalfe. No. 1 in the Series, Sand grain cover, Price 10p.

Churches and the Church by J.N. Darby. Edited. No. 2 in the Series, Sand grain cover, Price 10p.

The Ministers of Christ by John Metcalfe. No. 3 in the Series, Sand grain cover, Price 10p.

The Inward Witness by George Fox. Edited. No. 4 in the Series, Sand grain cover, Price 10p.

The Notion of a Clergyman by J.N. Darby. Edited. No. 5 in the Series, Sand grain cover, Price 10p.

The Servant of the Lord by William Huntington. Edited and Abridged. No. 6 in the Series, Sand grain cover, Price 10p.

One Spirit by William Kelly. Edited. No. 7 in the Series, Sand grain cover, Price 10p.

The Funeral of Arminianism by William Huntington. Edited and Abridged. No. 8 in the Series, Sand grain cover, Price 10p.

One Body by William Kelly. Edited. No. 9 in the Series, Sand grain cover, Price 10p.

False Churches and True by John Metcalfe. No. 10 in the Series, Sand grain cover, Price 10p.

Separation from Evil by J.N. Darby. Edited. No. 11 in the Series, Sand grain cover, Price 10p.

The Remnant by J.B. Stoney. Edited. No. 12 in the Series, Sand grain cover, Price 10p.

The Arminian Skeleton by William Huntington. Edited and Abridged. No. 13 in the Series, Sand grain cover, Price 10p.

FOUNDATION TRACTS

FOUNDATION TRACTS

1. **Female Priests?** by John Metcalfe. Oatmeal cover, price 25p.

2. **The Bondage of the Will** by Martin Luther. Translated and Abridged. Oatmeal cover, price 25p.

3. **Of the Popish Mass** by John Calvin. Translated and Abridged. Oatmeal cover, price 25p.

4. **The Adversary** by John Metcalfe. Oatmeal cover, price 25p.

MINISTRY BY JOHN METCALFE

TAPE MINISTRY BY JOHN METCALFE
FROM ENGLAND AND THE FAR EAST
IS AVAILABLE.

In order to obtain this free recorded ministry, please send your blank cassette (C.90) and the cost of the return postage, including your name and address in block capitals, to the John Metcalfe Publishing Trust, Church Road, Tylers Green, Penn, Bucks, HP10 8LN. Tapelists are available on request.

Owing to the increased demand for the tape ministry, we are unable to supply more than two tapes per order, except in the case of meetings for the hearing of tapes, where a special arrangement can be made.

THE MINISTRY OF THE NEW TESTAMENT

The purpose of this substantial A4 gloss paper magazine is to provide spiritual and experimental ministry with sound doctrine which rightly and prophetically divides the Word of Truth.

Readers of our books will already know the high standards of our publications. They can be confident that these pages will maintain that quality, by giving access to enduring ministry from the past, much of which is derived from sources that are virtually unobtainable today, and publishing a living ministry from the present. Selected articles from the following writers have already been included:

ELI ASHDOWN · ABRAHAM BOOTH · JOHN BRADFORD
JOHN BUNYAN · JOHN BURGON · JOHN CALVIN · DONALD CARGILL
JOHN CENNICK · J.N. DARBY · GEORGE FOX · JOHN FOXE
WILLIAM GADSBY · GREY HAZLERIGG · WILLIAM HUNTINGTON
WILLIAM KELLY · JOHN KENNEDY · JOHN KERSHAW · HANSERD KNOLLYS
JAMES LEWIS · MARTIN LUTHER · ROBERT MURRAY MCCHEYNE
JOHN METCALFE · ALEXANDER—SANDY—PEDEN · J.C. PHILPOT
J.K. POPHAM · JAMES RENWICK · J.B. STONEY · HENRY TANNER
ARTHUR TRIGGS · JOHN VINALL · JOHN WARBURTON
JOHN WELWOOD · GEORGE WHITEFIELD · J.A. WYLIE

Price £1.75 (postage included)
Issued Spring, Summer, Autumn, Winter.

Book Order Form

Please send to the address below:-

		Price	Quantity
A Question for Pope John Paul II		£1.25	......
Of God or Man?		£1.45	......
Noah and the Flood		£1.90	......
Divine Footsteps		£0.95	......
The Red Heifer		£0.75	......
The Wells of Salvation		£1.50	......
The Book of Ruth (Hardback edition)		£4.95	......
Divine Meditations of William Huntington		£2.35	......
Present-Day Conversions of the New Testament Kind		£2.25	......
Saving Faith		£2.25	......
Deliverance from the Law		£1.90	......
The Beatitudes		£1.90	......
Colossians		£0.95	......
Philippians		£1.90	......

Psalms, Hymns & Spiritual Songs (Hardback edition)

		Price	Quantity
The Psalms of the Old Testament		£2.50	......
Spiritual Songs from the Gospels		£2.50	......
The Hymns of the New Testament		£2.50	......

'Apostolic Foundation of the Christian Church' series

		Price	Quantity
Foundations Uncovered	Vol.I	£0.75	......
The Birth of Jesus Christ	Vol.II	£0.95	......
The Messiah (Hardback edition)	Vol.III	£7.75	......
The Son of God and Seed of David (Hardback edition)	Vol.IV	£6.95	......
Christ Crucified (Hardback edition)	Vol.V	£6.95	......
Justification by Faith (Hardback edition)	Vol.VI	£7.50	......
The Church: What is it? (Hardback edition)	Vol.VII	£7.75	......

Name and Address (in block capitals)

. . . .

. . . .

. . . .

If money is sent with order please allow for postage. Please address to:- The
John Metcalfe Publishing Trust, Church Road, Tylers Green, Penn, Bucks, HP10 8LN.

lvii

Tract Order Form

Please send to the address below:-

		Price	Quantity
Evangelical Tracts			
The Two Prayers of Elijah		£0.10	......
Wounded for our Transgressions		£0.10	......
The Blood of Sprinkling		£0.10	......
The Grace of God that Brings Salvation		£0.10	......
The Name of Jesus		£0.10	......
The Ministry of the New Testament		£0.10	......
The Death of the Righteous by A.M.S.		£0.10	......
Repentance		£0.10	......
Legal Deceivers Exposed		£0.10	......
Unconditional Salvation		£0.10	......
Religious Merchandise		£0.10	......
Comfort		£0.10	......
Peace		£0.10	......
Eternal Life		£0.10	......
'Tract for the Times' series			
The Gospel of God	No.1	£0.25	......
The Strait Gate	No.2	£0.25	......
Eternal Sonship and Taylor Brethren	No.3	£0.25	......
Marks of the New Testament Church	No.4	£0.25	......
The Charismatic Delusion	No.5	£0.25	......
Premillennialism Exposed	No.6	£0.25	......
Justification and Peace	No.7	£0.25	......
Faith or presumption?	No.8	£0.25	......
The Elect undeceived	No.9	£0.25	......
Justifying Righteousness	No.10	£0.25	......
Righteousness Imputed	No.11	£0.25	......
The Great Deception	No.12	£0.25	......
A Famine in the Land	No.13	£0.25	......
Blood and Water	No.14	£0.25	......
Women Bishops?	No.15	£0.25	......
The Heavenly Vision	No.16	£0.25	......

Name and Address (in block capitals)

. . . .

. . . .

. . . .

If money is sent with order please allow for postage. Please address to:- The
John Metcalfe Publishing Trust, Church Road, Tylers Green, Penn, Bucks, HP10 8LN.

cut here

Tract Order Form

Please send to the address below:-

		Price	Quantity
Ecclesia Tracts			
The Beginning of the Ecclesia	No.1	£0.10	......
Churches and the Church (J.N.D.)	No.2	£0.10	......
The Ministers of Christ	No.3	£0.10	......
The Inward Witness (G.F.)	No.4	£0.10	......
The Notion of a Clergyman (J.N.D.)	No.5	£0.10	......
The Servant of the Lord (W.H.)	No.6	£0.10	......
One Spirit (W.K.)	No.7	£0.10	......
The Funeral of Arminianism (W.H.)	No.8	£0.10	......
One Body (W.K.)	No.9	£0.10	......
False Churches and True	No.10	£0.10	......
Separation from Evil (J.N.D.)	No.11	£0.10	......
The Remnant (J.B.S.)	No.12	£0.10	......
The Arminian Skeleton (W.H.)	No.13	£0.10	......
Foundation Tracts			
Female Priests?	No.1	£0.25	......
The Bondage of the Will (Martin Luther)	No.2	£0.25	......
Of the Popish Mass (John Calvin)	No.3	£0.25	......
The Adversary	No.4	£0.25	......

Name and Address (in block capitals)

. . . .

. . . .

. . . .

If money is sent with order please allow for postage. Please address to:- The John Metcalfe Publishing Trust, Church Road, Tylers Green, Penn, Bucks, HP10 8LN.

Magazine Order Form

Name and Address (in block capitals)

. . . .

. . . .

. . . .

Please send me .... current copy/copies of The Ministry of the New Testament.

Please send me .... year/s subscription.

I enclose a cheque/postal order for £ ....

(Price: including postage, U.K. £1.75; Overseas £1.90)
(One year's subscription: Including postage, U.K. £7.00; Overseas £7.60)

Cheques should be made payable to The John Metcalfe Publishing Trust, and for overseas subscribers should be in pounds sterling drawn on a London Bank.

10 or more copies to one address will qualify for a 10% discount

Back numbers from Spring 1986 available.

Please send to The John Metcalfe Publishing Trust, Church Road, Tylers Green, Penn, Bucks, HP10 8LN

All Publications of the Trust are subsidised by the Publishers.